SPEAKING OF CHILDREN

SPEAKING
OF
CHILDREN

By

Elliott D. Landau

Published by Deseret Book Company
Salt Lake City, Utah
1975

For Herman and Bertha Landau,
my beloved Dad and Mom

contents

XIV

XIX

preface

The story is told of a man in an automobile who was following a truck down a very narrow road. Since it was impossible for him to go around the truck, he followed for quite a distance, looking for an opportunity to swing around in front.

Suddenly the truck stopped. The driver got out of his cab, reached for a two-by-four board, and beat upon the side of the truck. Then he climbed back into the driver's seat and continued for a few more miles before stopping again and repeating the process.

After a third time, the man in the car could contain his curiosity no longer. He got out of his car, went up to the truck driver, and said, "You know, I've been following you for miles and I can't for the life of me understand why you stop so often, get out, and beat the side of your truck like that. Would you mind explaining it?"

The truck driver turned to him and said, "Mister, this is a one-and-a-half-ton truck, and I'm carrying two tons of canaries. Every time I stop this truck and beat the side with this two-by-four, it keeps about half a ton of those canaries flying around. That way I'm not overloaded."

If anything truthful can be said about the American parent, it is indeed that at times he feels "overloaded." I spend a great share of my time reading newspapers, magazines, research reports, and other publications that focus upon children. I have learned that talking about them to parents is important. I have also learned that most parents feel terribly overloaded, and the purpose of this volume is not only to give you an idea about how other folks are doing, but also to assure you that almost everyone is in about the same boat.

While it is true that some knowledge helps in rearing children, it is also true that intuition and intellectual functioning can make a difference. If one combines the facts with intuition, sensitivity, and love, it need not be too difficult to rear a fine family.

Speaking of Children is another volume in a series of books based upon my one-minute radio programs. In a minute I can't say very much, but it *is* possible to make a point or two so that in your odd moments you may find an opportunity to browse and discuss and reflect. Happiness to you, and may this book, which talks about children, make a difference in your family.

acknowledgments

It takes many people to produce a book. All of them deserve thanks, but it should be understood that everything I have said here is my own responsibility.

I would like to acknowledge especially my own children and their mother for the at-home experiences that have added to whatever vision I bring to my readers.

I acknowledge also the many teachers and colleagues who have made an impression upon my thinking.

I am indebted to Bonneville International Corporation, whose nationwide facilities have carried these broadcasts daily. For Arch L. Madsen and his continued support, I am particularly grateful.

I am very pleased with the work of Lucas R. Visser of Total Design, who designed the book and has brought a certain penetrating vision to make my thoughts appear more graphic.

My thanks to Eleanor Knowles of Deseret Book for her editing, and to William James Mortimer, my publisher at Deseret Book, for his sustaining vote and cooperation in every step of the road. And finally, my appreciation to Deseret Book's board of directors, who approve each publication; their continued support and attention over the years have allowed me to break into print so that I might reach a larger audience.

INFANCY AND EARLY CHILDHOOD

infancy and early childhood (birth to five)

It would seem logical to start this book by talking about infancy and early childhood, and so that's where I have started. What follows is a selection of my thoughts about infancy and early childhood that have been broadcast nationwide during the past few years.

For some twenty years I have been pondering the true state of early childhood. On the one hand I have heard from colleagues throughout the nation that everything that's important happens to a child before he reaches the age of six. On the other hand we have heard that there is nothing that cannot be changed even after the age of six, ten, twenty-six, or forty-six. We have called the first five or six years of life the crucial years. Some have made the years appear to be so crucial that any dysfunction in those years has been considered to be the irrevocable downfall of the child.

At the present moment I should like to report that while I consider the early years very important, I have become convinced that any dynamic theory of human growth and development must consider the fact of the magnificent resiliency of the human organism. I believe that the die of life is not cast irrevocably or irretrievably in those earliest years. I rather hold that though these are crucial years, dysfunction in these years does not necessarily mean the dismal failure of the child in the future. In fact, I hold to the notion that throughout all of our lives we face crises we have gone through previously.

Dr. Erik Erikson has postulated in his "stages of life paradigm" that in the first year or so of life, the infant learns trust or mistrust. In the next few years of life he learns autonomy or doubt; and then in the years up until the age of five or six, initiative or guilt. I accept these designations as being a reasonable representation of what happens to us as we proceed from birth through the sixth year of life. It would seem obvious that were a child to be brought up in these years with a great deal of trust, autonomy, and initiative, he would enter his school years and his life to follow with a giant head start. On the other hand, should a child's life and circumstances in these first years be composed of mistrust, doubt, and the feelings of guilt, then we would assume that the youngster would enter school and the rest of his life greatly handicapped. It seems to me that these formulations are true. Trust, autonomy, and initiative in liberal amounts produce the more confident youngster, while mistrust, doubt, and guilt produce a child with a poor self-image.

a happy mother

4 But I am persuaded that the organism known as the human being can absorb a modicum of mistrust, doubt, and guilt in the first five or six years of life, and while he will be handicapped in the future, that handicap is not irremediable. In other words, I believe that because of the mistakes, and on occasion the confusion, that exist in parents' minds, a child can be brought up with a dose of these negative experiences and yet in the succeeding stages of his life overcome them.

It is for those parents who really worry that they've caused irremediable damage that this section of my book is meant. The chances are you have *not* caused such damage. But if like the rest of us you have erred on occasion, be assured that human beings have a great capacity for suffering. When children know their parents love and respect them, they are able to weather lapses of parental perfection. If the basic message of acceptance has been transmitted, an occasional garble won't ruin the text. Cheer up!

It seems clear that the single most important factor in the healthy emotional growth of a child during the first five years of his life is the degree of marital happiness his mother is experiencing. A mother who is dissatisfied with her marriage is more likely to bring up an infantalized child than one who is enjoying her married life. When a mother is definitely unhappy, she tends to lavish attention on her children so that they cannot develop a sense of self and a degree of wholesome autonomy or independence, factors vital to the further growth of the child. A mother's mental state has its influence on the child even when it is still unborn, so it is easy to see how the state of happiness of the mother can affect the child after its birth. An emotionally healthy mother takes life as it is: she rolls with the punches, she aggressively attacks life and finds no need to discover her happiness through loving her infant to death. An unhappy marriage is never a pleasant thing; its consequences upon the normal and desirable growth of the children of that marriage are tragic and tragically unnecessary.

what children must love

a great home environment

There are two kinds of love a child needs to cultivate. The first is a love for himself. In fact, before a child can love others, he must love himself. A child's love of himself depends very much on how others who are significant in his life see him. If they show their love to him, especially in his earliest years, he begins to see himself as being loved. Children need to feel verbal and nonverbal love from others; then when they have felt sufficiently good about themselves, they are able to turn that love in the direction of others. This is the second kind of love that eventually produces a whole person. Children often love things or objects with such passion that their loss seems to be the end of the world. For this they ought not to be made ashamed. When a child can mourn the loss of something he has learned to love, he has learned the lesson most important to furthering his sharing in the good life. Mourning is part of loss, and sorrow helps us grow. What children love, they need to pursue. This is healthy and should be encouraged.

There are three major aims of a successful home environment in relation to the rearing of youngsters: First, all efforts to change behavior in children should be done with positive motivation; that is, we need to avoid deprecating the child to change him. Second, each child needs to feel some measure of daily success so that he goes to bed each evening feeling better about his capacities and performance. Third, self-direction and personal responsibility are the ultimate aims of all parent-child relationships. Ah, you must be saying to yourself, how nice if only I could always be like that. Well, you can't always be uplifting, positive, and so skillful that the child feels success daily. But you can more frequently watch what you say and do, and start to move in this direction. I can almost guarantee changed behavior on your part if you will simply catch yourself and pre-plan what you will say and do before you say or do it.

5

six ways to have healthy babies

midwives again!

6 Virginia Apgar, in her book *Is My Baby Right?,* gives the following sound advice to prospective parents. First, a hereditary condition in the family means that the parents ought to get genetic counseling. Second, it is best for a woman to have her children between the ages of twenty and thirty-five, with at least two years between the end of one pregnancy and the beginning of another. Third, no woman should become pregnant unless she has had the German measles or has been immunized against it. During pregnancy she should do everything possible to avoid exposure to contagious diseases. Next, she should avoid undercooked meat and contact with cats who have eaten such meat. Fifth, a pregnant woman should not be exposed to X-rays or take any drugs except as directed by a physician who knows she is pregnant. Finally, cigarettes are a no-no. Is all of this a flat guarantee? It isn't, but it will go a long way to increase a couple's chances of not having a child with a handicap. If you need to know more, consult your obstetrician or health clinic. It pays.

It is good to hear about a program designed to bring back some of the flavor of the past when a woman could have a baby without some male physician poking about. The midwife is back, and there are some 1,200 accredited nurses with two years of additional experience behind them who are helping relieve the shortage of trained obstetricians. American obstetricians are overworked, and it is the experience of many women that little personal attention is given. Besides, there isn't a man who can really feel for a woman in labor. Pregnancy is not an illness. True, over the years untrained women delivered most of the babies and the mortality was phenomenal. Let us not take anything away from this nearly all-male profession. It has made having a baby a lot safer than it was in Grandma's day. Those who believe more in natural childbirth, without the sterility of keeping husbands and family away from the site of delivery, enjoy midwives because they are far more liberal about who and where the baby gets delivered. Eighty percent of the babies born into the world today are delivered by midwives, even in such technologically advanced places as England, West Germany, the Netherlands, and Scandinavia.

u.s. infant mortality

baby pollution?

It has long been my assumption that all children in the world are equally precious no matter what their color or creed. I cannot merely shrug when I hear of children starving in Biafra or Salonika. I am somewhat amazed at those who simply figure that if the children aren't Americans, they somehow get used to hunger or disease. After all, you can only die from starvation once. I have often looked at our nation and beamed inside a bit when I thought of how safe it was for babies. Imagine my chagrin when I learned recently that the risk of an American infant dying during the first year of life is greater than at any other year until he is 65. There are fifteen nations in the world where it is safer to be born and where the first year of life is less hazardous than in America. And if by chance you are nonwhite and living in America, if you are black, Indian, Chicano, or a host of other color possibilities, the infant mortality death rate is 64 percent greater. Shall we only be first in war, weapons, and the production of cars?

The last word about bearing and rearing children will never be said, it seems. It is always safe to stay away from areas in which people feel very personally involved. I do not attempt to advocate any particular side of the controversy about limiting families. I am not personally persuaded about any kind of necessity about either extreme—zero population growth or unbridled multiplication. The really basic question is not economic or ecological. It is and always will be whether or not any particular family can produce fine, sane, happy, and productive children. Brilliant families or affluent ones are not the criterion. Half a dozen children born and then raised with loving care, with intelligence and concern, might be less polluters of the environment than the one child born into different circumstances. To say that too many children will pollute the planet has always seemed to me to be an oversimplification of the problem. It is not how many but what quality of human will enter this world that matters. Enough people will limit their families if they allow others to choose their own path. No one ought to feel guilty about having children who are loved and wanted.

spacing babies

looking at infants

⑧ Let us get a few things straight about babies, family planning, and rivalries between children. Parents who love each other and delight in creative family living will raise happy kids no matter how they are or are not spaced—but too many of us are not these people. If you have made up you mind that you *will* space your children, however, there are some things you ought to know. First, you will never cut out any sibling rivalry with a predetermined spacing such as two or three years between children. In fact, there isn't much wrong with child rivalry, because it produces strength through turmoil. It rarely paralyzes growth, but it can cause trauma. Once again, I am not here to take any side with regard to spacing, having had my own two years apart for an eight-year period of time. But, if you insist, three years seems to be ideal when everything is taken into consideration. That is, the risk of premature birth and associated birth defects is higher when there is little spacing. If spacing is too close, the drain upon the emotional health of the mother and family is more serious. If children are born too far apart, however, you are really raising two only children. Happy babies to one and all—spaced or unspaced.

We shall now have a look at what some newborns look like and why they do some of the things they do. Most new babies do not look like the romantic pictures of three-month-old children you will see in magazines. Instead, their faces are often puffy and somewhat bluish, their eyelids swollen. When a light is shined into their eyes, they blink. Swelling eyelids are due to the fact that they have been head down just prior to delivery. It is also possible that swollen eyelids protect the babies from too much sight stimulation in their first days on earth. From the beginning infants do fix on and track a bright object if it moves slowly. Crying also serves a real purpose. It isn't just to drive new mothers crazy. It helps children fill their lungs and open the tiny airspaces in their lungs to get rid of fluid that has been there for some time. Their purple color comes from their unaerated lungs, and though their feet and hands may remain blue for weeks, they will eventually become pink all over. They are wonders, miracles of mechanism, and a handful...sometimes a nightful, too.

babies prepare to be born

newborn reactions

While reading a newspaper in Auckland, New Zealand, I was interested in a report on the research work of Professor G. C. Liggins of the Auckland University School of Medicine. He reports that in the latter part of pregnancy babies spend several hours a day practicing for birth. During dream sleep they practice gulping down fluid in preparation for breast-feeding; they practice breathing movements in anticipation of the work they will have to do on their own after birth; and they develop a sense of taste and smell. In fact, Professor Liggins states that some functions performed by developing babies in the fetal stages would leave a highly qualified engineer dumbfounded. Babies are actually able to ensure that their lungs inflate properly at birth by developing special linings around lung air sacks to keep lungs under pressure as they fill with air. Babies also store up special fat to keep them insulated at birth. They exercise lung and chest muscles in the last four or five weeks of pregnancy. The research indicates that in these weeks the baby, not the mother, is in control of most events related to preparation for birth.

We have traditionally viewed infancy with a great deal of nostalgia and apathy. Almost any mother will tell you that in the first few weeks of life her baby sleeps most of the time. And yet, research studies show that the activity level displayed by a child in the first three days of life is far greater than predicted and more intense than anything that happens in the month to follow. For whatever reason, the newborn's reaction to his new nonembryonic environment is unusually alert and responsive, even more so than physicians had thought. It is particularly interesting to learn that infants cared for in nurseries during the first three days of life differentiate between day and night far less than children brought up by their natural or surrogate mothers. All of this adds further fuel to the evidence that suggests that babies thrive when given close maternal-like care in their earliest days of life.

try breast feeding

of babies, bottles, and breast feeding

10 The controversy about breast-feeding is in the limelight again. This time the *British Medical Journal* reports that mother's milk not only provides babies with protective antibodies against childhood infection but also gives protection against certain diseases that afflict adults. Adults who were breast-fed as babies have been found to be comparatively free of such common modern adult ailments as high blood pressure, hardening of the arteries, and obesity. In formula-fed babies there is a statistically significant amount of baby ailments that are not found in others who are breast-fed. Statistically significant means that the differences between the two groups are large enough that no chance or little chance factor could have played any significant part. Formula-fed babies suffer a proportionately greater share of problems with eczema and asthma, ulcerative colitis, and arteriosclerosis. Even breast-feeding for the first few weeks seems to affect infant deaths from blood clots. The author of the journal article recommends breast-feeding exclusively for at least three months, and a continuation for at least six months will help baby off to a good head start.

Doctors are often asked whether or not it is possible to bring home a new baby and avoid the often intense rivalry between the new arrival and the older child at home. Frequently the trouble bubbles over during the feeding time of the new baby, and some mothers mistakenly believe that it is their breast-feeding that fans the flames of discontent and jealousy in the older sibling. There seems to be no evidence whatever that this is true, so I'd encourage mothers to breast-feed if they can. The feeling of being left out will occur anyway. When bottle-feeding their babies, mothers feeling particularly guilty will often prop the bottle and pay attention to the older child. This is a cold, sterile way to feed and should be avoided until the baby is at least a year old. I've seen mothers bring the older sibling onto their laps with them whether they are breast- or bottle-feeding. Sure it's tough on junior, but he'll survive. Give him plenty of attention when baby is sleeping, and all will be well.

feeding babies solids

eating problems

There was a time when no baby got a morsel of solid food for at least three months. Then came the revolution, and they were started on solid food in the second or third week of life. The assumption was that solid food produced faster growth, which in turn enabled the baby to sleep through the night earlier and easier. I have a notion that this was not because it was good for babies but because it was good for parents who needed more sleep. Some physicians now seem to be saying that too much protein intake before three months can lead to intellectual impairment. It has been found that prepared baby foods have high salt levels and that this salt content is linked to the onset of early susceptibility to high blood pressure. Allergists and nutritionists are thinking that too early an introduction of solid foods may expose allergy-prone infants to a variety of allergens before they have the defenses to deal with them. The nutritionists are thinking that overfed infants are programmed for later obesity. So I'd consult that pediatrician and do what you both think best. My bets go with Mother Nature, who never intended children to eat solids before a long diet of mother's milk.

It has always been one of the hard and fast rules of child rearing that mothers are to blame if their children are problem eaters. However, some very recent studies of twins may contradict this old rule. If it is mother's anxiety over feeding that really causes finicky eaters, then both twins should become problem eaters. Since twins share in identical heredity, there are no striking differences in twin behavior. But in the matters of fussy eating, spitting up, and refusing certain types of foods, this study seems to show that there are minor differences in twins' eating habits, and thus their parents did not have the expected exact influence on the children. The researchers go on to stress that these problems in eating should be taken a bit more seriously, since a child can restrict his own diet to his nutritional detriment. My advice is, don't be upset by firm refusals about certain foods, but if the foods are really important, find substitutes the child may enjoy. And remember, few children starve to death if offered a variety of food.

malnutrition and   colicky babes

12 It is now a fact that two-thirds of the world's preschool children suffer from malnutrition. It is also a fact that deprivation of the protein and other substances found in good diets causes a retardation in growth and permanently damages health. It has already been suggested that it is highly probable that the low I.Q.s of slum children are not alone the result of meager experiences in childhood, but can be directly attributed to deficient protein diets that simply retard the proliferation of brain cells. All of this is especially tragic in view of the fact that in most of the European world there are heavy surpluses of milk. There is abundant evidence that hunger causes vagueness, loss of memory, irritability, poor concentration, hallucinations—all of which adds up to a pretty poor teaching candidate. I have personally faced hundreds of children in schools where the listless looks, gray faces, and quick tempers could be attributable to nothing but hunger and permanent malnutrition. Absalom, Absalom, where does our money go?

I will never forget the endless hours of walking the floors with our first baby, one hand mangling Spock, the other holding the squealing infant who is now eighteen. We had a charming French pediatrician who counseled that such infant behavior was perfectly normal and that at the end of three months it would all be over—and you know, it was. Meanwhile he called this *colic* and suggested that if we would dunk our forefingers in some commercial, bottled spirits and let the baby lap some of the distilled liquid, the cries would taper. Nothing helped but time. Since then I have studied colicky babies in the literature of childhood and have concluded that colic is due to a variety of things. For example, it could be due to the child being a firstborn, with new parenthood as the cause—but our fourth child wasn't much different! Two psychiatrists from Colorado now say that the three-month crying jag is to ensure the child's attachment to its parents. Well, ours was certainly attached to us. It seems quite possible that the intense crying is a demand for closeness and recognition. Whether it is or isn't, there isn't much any of us can do but grin and bear it.

sudden infant death syndrome

"bad start" babies

Every year at least 10,000 children in the second or third month of life are diapered, fed, burped, and put to bed. In the cold of morning the child is found scrunched up in a corner of the bed—dead. No one knows why. Such a tragedy tears parents apart. They feel guilt, remorse, anxiety, and hatred. Sudden infant death syndrome is the leading killer of children between the ages of one week and one year and the second most important cause of death, behind accidents, for children under fifteen. As of this moment a virus is suspected. How it works no one knows. What happens in many places throughout the country is that parents are left hopeless and helpless before the law that holds a coroner's inquest and all the trappings that go along with criminal proceedings. The emotional aftermath is cruel to parents who have already suffered. In many cities reams of health workers visit the families of children who died from sudden infant death syndrome and help them to survive their tragedy well. What they don't know can't hurt them.

There are such things as "bad start" babies. These are the children who are born prematurely or with defects or those who had mothers who had poor prenatal or poor delivery care that resulted in birth injuries. Modern pediatrics and psychiatry view the first six months of a child's life as crucial to his overall growth and development. Babies who had a bad start are particularly vulnerable to both physical and mental disturbances. In the opinion of Dr. Lois Murphy of Children's Hospital, Washington, D.C., the quality of life in the first six months is so important that an infant who has a bad start needs to be seen by a professional once a week for at least six months. When internal physical problems are not recognized and treated, the underlying physical, emotional, and intellectual development suffers and often persists through the growing years. In the first six months a child's mental structures and perceptions are being formed, and physical disability can retard these.

13

pacifiers and thumb-sucking

reinforcing thumb-sucking

14 Well, the battle over pacifiers for children is still raging. A classic report that studied 1,258 children between the years 1952 and 1971 has just been completed at the University of Toronto. Forty percent of all children in the study sucked their thumbs at one time or another, but children who were given a pacifier after weaning sucked their thumbs considerably less. While children are still on the breast or bottle, it is wise to avoid the pacifier. Too often it is shoved into junior's mouth just to shut him up. If a pacifier is so used, a dependence upon it grows and a thumb-sucker is made. It is important, too, if you get hung up on the pacifier that you keep a very small supply and that when one is broken or lost you lament the fact, and that is that. One of our children dropped his pacifier out of the car. We kissed it goodbye and never used another again. The study also showed that children from large families, from professional families, and from those who had prolonged weaning periods sucked their thumbs more. Finally, at age twelve, 20 percent of the thumb-suckers were still at it.

If you have a thumb-sucker at home, you will want to read something about this relatively harmless habit that excites parents more than anything else except toilet training. Parental concern about thumb-sucking usually ends up with the parent nagging, nagging about the habit time and time again, until the child is beautifully reinforced for the habit so reviled by the adults in his life. Making a big deal about the habit fixates it or insures that it will not go away. Perhaps worse than guaranteeing that the habit will be maintained is the fact that when parents continually refer to it, they do damage to the child's concept of self because all of the parental pressure convinces him not that they dislike his habit, but rather reject him. Only 1 percent of children suck their thumbs long enough to cause dental problems. Eighty-seven percent will stop by age three of their own accord. Another 10 percent or more will stop by age five. Worse than thumb-sucking for teeth is tongue-thrusting and mouth-breathing, both of which are treatable. So, let junior suck away even if it hurts your adult self-image. It won't hurt his teeth much.

the child's imagination

let 'em be

When a child is in his earliest preschool years, about two or three, the whole world is controlled by his imagination. It is an age when whatever he wishes to have happen occurs. And it is also a time when parents hold their heads and are heard to moan that the child is a liar and sorcerer and all manner of evil things. Of course, what parents are really saying is that the child's imagination is more than they can bear in their own world of reality. The story is told of a little boy who told his mother there was a bear outside the window. The mother protested that this couldn't be, so the child insisted further, finally insisting that the mother look outside the window. Upon doing this, mother saw a large black dog outside and, considering the child a deliberate liar, demanded that he go and pray to God for forgiveness for his lies. This the good child did. Then he returned, saying, ''Oh, Mother, it was quite all right. God heard what I said and told me not to worry because he has often mistaken Rover for a bear himself.'' And so it goes. Imagination is funny; it can do and does almost anything in the child's world.

I was watching a mother the other day who had two very young preschool-age children at home, and as I watched I thought of how much more she could do for these children if she could remember a few things. First, until a child signals that he needs help, let him do it alone. Her older boy was putting the pieces of a puzzle together, and the second he made a poor move, his mother was there to support him. The delight of trial and error and the eventual solution to the problem was denied him because his mother thought she was doing him good. Next, opposite the TV there was a coffee table that was just high enough for a child to sit comfortably on. It was wooden, sturdy, and really an excellent seat. But no was all Mom said to her child's attempt to sit on the table. I don't think it really makes much difference to a child where he sits, and there is very little about sitting on a low table that will destroy his character so early. Let him live and do things for himself. Parents, stay out and be quiet more than you are.

balancing freedom and restraint

limitations to growth

16

As in so many things, the key to success is a reasonable degree of order and restraint and a reasonable degree of freedom. I don't often allude to Ann Landers and her column, but a recent letter from a twenty-year-old did catch my eye. The young fellow complained that he lived with "showcase" parents. They demanded that their home, his room, and everything about their environment be kept so sparkling and neat that they could be proud if someone dropped in unexpectedly. When young children, especially before school starts, are not allowed to be children, not allowed to have messy fingers, not allowed to touch unless they are spotless, they can grow up with a desire to thwart their parents as they grow older. I'm not trying to say that children ought to destroy the looks of their home. I am pleading for an understanding of the fact that children don't see walls and mirrors in quite the same light that their adult-conscious parents might. Children need to grow in reasonable freedom and with a parental understanding that messy kids are not agents of the devil. Even what seems to be deliberate messiness is often not perceived by the child as such.

All human beings, especially children, have certain limitations upon their growth and development. In an era when we talk very seriously about the fullest development of human potential, it might be well to review what precisely are the limiting factors in children's lives. Children are limited by their physiology, their nutrition, their condition of body. Next, a lack of opportunity can seriously hamper growth. Earl Kelley used to say, "Whenever we start to worry about the next generation, we need to remind ourselves that they were all right when we got them." A third limitation on our full growth is the different human needs we each have. Higher needs cannot be met until lower, more basic needs, such as opportunity and physiology, are met. Human failure, maladjustment, stupidity, and criminality are often the consequences of not having needs met. Finally, we are limited in progression by our concept of ourselves. The most important single factor in progress is how we view ourselves in our attempts to progress.

children's fears

fear of the dentist

Some advice for parents who live in earthquake-prone areas. After the severe quakes in the San Fernando Valley, it was found that what children feared most was not being injured or even killed but separation from their parents. Some of the worst moments occurred when parents left children alone for a few moments to search for flashlights and candles. When parents went to assess the damage and left the child or children alone, this caused deep concern. It is good practice in times of natural catastrophes to not leave the children even momentarily, but rather to grope together, in the dark if need be. It is important in an emergency for the entire family to stay together. Parents' fears of the quakes caused children to be very fearful, but letting the children know that there is no shame to fear is considered to be very important. After a quake it is urgent not to just forget about it, because the fears still linger and need to be safely voiced by the children. And if children revert to earlier habits, such as thumb-sucking, for awhile, parents should consider this natural.

To many grown-ups the mere mention of the dentist starts a certain rigor mortis of the emotions due to abject fear. When children's drawings were studied to discover what they perceived their dentist to be, it was pretty clear that they saw dentists as sadistic fiends who operated torture chambers. It is important to recognize that children's fears are caught from the life around them, and they often seem rather ludicrous in the light of reality. But fears are very real to all of us, and they need to be approached as if they were quite factual. It really doesn't matter much how children catch their fears; what does matter is that these fears are paralyzing and traumatic enough to last for a lifetime. Thus we see explained how our adult fears are nurtured. The best advice for dentists is precisely what we have talked about before. Accept the reality of fear, acknowledging the child's feelings, and be ever so gentle.

grief is good

learning trust

18 It is healthy for a child to grieve over the death of a pet. Many parents unwittingly replace the dead dog or turtle so as to assuage the grief of the child. Yet it is a fact that grief is important because it provides time to regroup the child's feelings and to realize that attachment and loss are part of the realistic way of life. Too rapid replacement of a dead pet tells the child that all things are replaceable —including himself. The right way to recover properly from the death of a pet is to feel it, talk about it, and bring the grief to the surface, not bury it in make-believe play. I do not believe in absolute truth to all children. Where a child under six may suffer from a knowledge of the necessity to put his puppy to sleep because of imminent death, he should be lied to, with few or no feelings of guilt on the adults' part. To a child under the age of six, the putting to death of a beloved pet is inexplicable and only breeds abject fear of the child's own demise should he become ill. Truth liberates, but truth to those who cannot fathom it may imprison.

In a recent newspaper interview I talked about the importance of children saying no to their parents. After all, growing up is a process of becoming more and more independent. While independence is a highly prized trait as children grow, it is, in two-year-olds, an undesirable way of behaving. A two-year-old who too easily leaves his mother's side is quite probably showing some evidence of mistrusting his parents. In a recent talk Dr. Agnes Plenk of Salt Lake City suggested that a relationship of complete trust at age two is essential. A child who does not trust an adult at this tender age is likely to be hindered in his intellectual and emotional growth. For this type of child, one who is overly independent, it is important that he be put back on the road of developing trust by being given the daily close contact with one adult who really cares. Children who don't trust their parents at two have frequently had a series of bad experiences with these parents or with other adults who have in some way disappeared when they were most needed.

children need conflict

choices and children

The opinion of Dr. Rene Spitz regarding the kinds of things that happen to children who are reared with no conflict early in their lives is very interesting. Dr. Spitz's definition of conflict is simple. Children who are raised with a sensible series of no's in their lives are, in fact, being brought up with the right kind of conflict. Conflict does not mean violence, however. It would appear that Spitz was proposing that in all of us there is a need for a conflict with authority. If this need is not met through the daily interactions with parents, then it is likely to really erupt during adolescence. The resistance parents offer to the needs and wants of children is a maturing experience for the child. Children who do essentially what they wish to do, when they want to do it, are being deprived of a growing experience. It could be that the children who today are beating up teachers were those who ran the show at home before school started. Healthy no's never hurt; they develop the child's sense of right and wrong.

Paul Friedberg, a playground designer, said, "Give me *one* choice, and I'll bore myself to death, and I'll grow up to be a very narrow person. Give me a million choices, and you feed my imagination, my understanding of forms, of balance, of movement, and the playing becomes both a physical and an intellectual challenge, a learning by trial and error, and an experience of discovery and exploration." Too many parents and school people don't really believe in childhood, so they settle for one game, one type of playground with no choices, one reading program with no alternatives. It is a demonstrable fact that the brain increases in weight and in its ability to operate as it exists in a varied environment. Hamburger every day is dull. The same set of playground equipment with nothing else to do is dull. Young children's environments should be visually and aesthetically stimulating. Children thrive by doing lots of things so that their imaginations get stretched.

19

coloring books   children's toys

The favorite method of keeping kids quiet, next to TV, of course, is the coloring book. It is not an evil thing; it simply is not in any form, shape, or manner what an art experience ought to be. Coloring books, like the adult counterpart, the paint-by-numbers kit, allow children to color what someone else has drawn. I have been amazed at both children and adults who actually frame these do-it-by-number things and then claim to have drawn them. In a society that should know fraud from authenticity, one can imagine children growing up not really knowing what their own creations are. Art should provide an outlet for feelings, for the creative urge, for awareness of self, for personal observations of life, both in fact and fancy. Where can a coloring book help in these vital realms? Keeping within boundary lines in art is of little importance, and you may be assured that children will not learn obedience from a coloring book. But them some large butcher paper, and give them space and time. Goodbye to coloring mania!

While many children have all of the advantages of puzzles, toys, games, and the like, there are too many who, because of an excess of manufactured toys, don't have the opportunity to simply creatively amuse themselves. The chance to work creatively with paint, clay, paper, scissors, paste, and crayons is often neglected when it is so easy to buy prefabricated toys. Yet it is precisely the experience of doing the unstructured that is so healthy for the growing child's mind. The intuitive part of the mind, the imaginative experience, cannot be underestimated. What happens as children play with the formless, the unmanufactured, is just what stays with them for the rest of their lives. To make a four-wheeled thing go or to fit together shapes that someone else has already predetermined is a rather low-level type of activity compared to creation with materials that are nothing at first and become something because the child has done it. Increasing one's sensitivity, awareness, and flexibility is a priceless activity. Look less for the toy and more for the materials that will expand the child's real powers.

early schooling

early education in new zealand

If I haven't made my position clear so far on early schooling for children, then I shall state it here with equivocation. I see no evidence, neurologically, educationally, or in any other dimension related to child growth and development, that persuades me that there is any real point to formally educating children starting at age four. In fact, the evidence is overwhelming that children dislike school when they start early. Much learning theory indicates that formal learning should be delayed, not accelerated; that neurologically the eyes and brain are not ready for many formal-type learnings. For instance, if four-year-olds are taught to read, and in cases this can be done, there is discomfort with close vision. There is a lack of discrimination between letters that look alike. The eye is not the reader; the brain is. The brain matures at its own pace, and much hard evidence exists that it isn't ready at four for formal operations such as arithmetic and reading. We would be well-advised to let the home and family be the center of learning and attention. The teacher is ready, willing, and able to take the six-year-old onward at the proper pace.

I want to tell you about New Zealand's system of early childhood education that really makes great sense to me. In nearly every community or subdivision there must, by law, be set aside enough land by the developer for a kiddie school that will serve the community. These are somewhat smallish, well-kept houses that usually contain two large rooms with a place for children to play indoors and outdoors. And, of course, the teachers have to have their tearoom, where they can instantly boil oodles of water to help them survive the day. I think that the most memorable parts of these schools are the kiddie toilets, each with toilet bowls built for children—not the white castles that our children, no matter how small, have to mount in order to celebrate their bodily functions. I am excited at the concept of community planning that forces people to set aside space for the education of young people. Rich or poor, everyone in New Zealand has equal access to some fine playschools for three-year-olds.

day-care nurseries

ideal day-care centers

22 The day-care nursery idea is not likely to simmer down as we move toward an economy where mothers and fathers are both breadwinners. Child-care experts agree that the best place, the ideal place, for a child to be in his preschool years is at home. Research by many experts shows that the best place to stimulate a child to think, to try, to research and discover is at home with his mother. Children need more than just feeding and diapering. Whatever smacks of institutionalism usually results in a sterile, canned environment. Too often today when there are some exemplary day-care centers, we find that the cards have been stacked in favor of a total environment that is accepting, stimulating, and altogether captivating. Mothers are not the only ones, we hear, who can do good things for children. Concerned, empathetic strangers can provide nearly everything a child needs. Ideally, a child's mother is the best one to provide the best environment. If I were sure that mass day-care would ever get to be more than feeding and diapering, I'd okay it. It won't and I can't.

Day-care centers for young children are usually a pretty hot topic because there are those who know that children must not be just dumped into heated centers and then left to the care of folks who are undereducated and underpaid. Ideally, the day-care center should be an extension of the family and become part of what has been termed a "constellation of mothering." Any attempt to simply provide custodial care, such as 99 percent of preschool centers do presently, is ill advised. There is a tremendous body of literature that rather clearly indicates that the American marriage is failing. It is in too many ways disintegrating badly, what with divorces, separations, and the many unhappy marriages. Day-care for children needs to be the kind that will upgrade family life. We commit grave error in thinking that just because many marriages fail, it must follow that the institution of the family is a failure too. The day-care center must become a model for families and, in fact, become an educative experience for both children and adults.

children and women's lib

parents and early reading

Not long ago a women's lib specialist advocated that professional women need to have practical mothers available who would take children from their real mothers at the age of a few months so that the highly trained professionals could go back to their high-powered jobs. After the children reach the age of two, a day-care nursery would take over. I have a few simple questions here for our liberationist female friends. One is, how is it that a movement devoted to liberating females accepts so casually the development of a whole class of women good only for child rearing? Second, if children are to be managed intelligently, why do these women want any children at all? The literature of the women's lib movement has, in the words of Professor Adelson of Michigan, "no place in it at all for children." He says it is something like sex in the Victorian novel, "invisible, unmentionable, taboo." Our middle class is muddled enough with children who claim their parents gave them everything they needed but nothing they wanted. We need more love and care for children, not less.

Most reading experts agree that nearly any mother can do much at home to develop an interest in words in her pre-school-age children. All it takes is ten minutes a day, sitting down with an open newspaper, magazine, or catalogue, looking through it, talking about the pictures, reading out loud, and asking the child to point to parts of the picture and then circle them or draw a line under them. Here's a typical exchange between parent and child: "Joe, draw a circle around the man's shoe; now color his tie or hat. Next, name the machine he has near him to cut the grass, and tell me the color of the blouse the girl is wearing." Looking for a specific object is good practice in listening and following directions. Asking for colors gives practice in naming and matching and comparing. Not the least benefit of all of this is the ten minutes of concentrated attention your child will get from his very busy mother. He'll love it and so will you, if you keep it fun and keep it up.

23

criticizing sesame street

"no" on sesame

For the most part the television series *Sesame Street* has received the plaudits of nearly everyone. But like all things that are part of the public offering, it is subject to a share of criticism. Let's review what it is the people in front of the screen object to. Major criticism comes from sources that object to the choppy, rapid nature of the program, which discourages the development of attention span, says Helen Bech, preschool specialist. She further states that the letters and numbers jumping out of the screen are a form of oral agression against children. To both of these criticisms all I can say is, "So what?" I don't think anyone should expect an educational miracle from any one source. Other critics say that *Sesame Street* encourages only passive learning that doesn't last. Another report says that *Sesame's* ideas are based upon the psychology of the TV commercial, in that children are brainwashed by clever illustrations of great intensity, form, and speed. Well, it is easy to play armchair general when the other fellow has gone into battle. *Sesame Street* makes most TV for children look like amateur theatricals.

Herbert Sprigle has been a consistently vocal critic of the darling of TV for preschool children, *Sesame Street*. *Sesame Street's* avowed objective was to do two things: (1) prepare poverty children better for first-grade experiences, and (2) narrow the achievement gap between poor youngsters and middle-class children. His two studies indicate neither of these two things happened. His earlier study compared twenty-four children who were classified as poverty children and who had attended a kindergarten using *Sesame Street* programs, curriculum, and materials as its educational component, with twenty-four poverty children who attended the same school, had the same teachers, but used no TV and no *Sesame Street* program or materials. After three weeks of first grade he gave each group the Metropolitan Reading Test and concluded that *Sesame*-trained children were no better prepared for first grade than the other youngsters. In fact, their scores tended to be lower. At the end of first grade, the Stanford Achievement Test used on both groups showed no significant difference whatever.

"yes" on sesame   what's on tv?

Dr. Herbert Sprigle says that *Sesame Street* hasn't lived up to its claims regarding the intellectual and emotional development of poor children. On the other hand, Sam Ball and Gerry Bogatz of the Educational Testing Service reached very different conclusions. Their findings indicate a very positive effect of the program on the intellectual progress of both disadvantaged and middle-class children. In fact, their recommendation is that the program be geared more for three-year-olds than fours and fives so that the intellectual potential of these children might be tapped. I have made no detailed analyses of either of these experiments, so I must defer judgment. But I have just finished watching *Sesame Street* in living color, and here is what I think: Regardless of its intent, it is as captivating, energetic, and sparkling as it ever was. Its underlying messages are clear and clever. It respects childhood because it encourages pathos. Neither it nor the *Electric Company,* which is too staccato for my taste, ought or need to expect learning gains to accrue to justify its existence.

At the annual meeting of the American Academy of Pediatrics, Dr. Gerald Looney reported that the prekindergarten child spends more than 60 percent of his waking time before a TV set. By the time he goes to kindergarten, the child will have devoted more hours to TV watching than a student spends in four years of college. A *Christian Science Monitor* survey recorded that in 74 hours of prime-time viewing during one week, there were 217 incidents and threats of violence and 125 killings and murders in full view of the TV audience. Finally, the Arizona studies found that by the age of fourteen a child has seen 18,000 humans killed on TV. By the time a student gets through high school, he or she has seen 350,000 commercials, many of them of dubious content or value. Let's not throw out the baby with the bath water. TV is one of man's greatest achievements. Let's just be certain that in commercial TV programs the finest materials for children be included during prime time, and that some percentage of their budget be used for non-commercial support of such programming.

selling to kids on tv

children and books

26 Kidvid is the name given to children's TV programs by the people who produce these programs. Lately there has been some criticism of kidvid commercials. A child who watches from eight A.M. Saturday morning to one P.M. will see 100 commercials, mostly for cold cereals, candy, and toys. Is this good or bad? One group says that these are unfair selling methods because the sophistication of the commercial messages is more than children can cope with. This group, Action for Children's Television (ACT), says that it is unethical to hard-sell children. Just because a product looks or feels good doesn't necessarily say it is good. On the opposite side of the argument, the TV industry and advertisers claim that there is no real harm proven and that commercials are part of a child's consumer education. As I see it, commercials for children are okay provided advertisers are scrupulous about the truth and provided they advertise only that which is reasonably beneficial to the growth and development of children. I think industry has the right to sell, but their record with truth in advertising is less than impressive, and children are too young to tell the difference.

Children who watch *Sesame Street* learn many concepts of size, shape, and numbers. This they do without any adult help. But when a TV program is followed up by a mother reviewing what they both saw and hear, the results are even better. I am pleased to report that when children, especially those whose homes do not provide much experience in the standard English dialect, are read to from children's books every day, and when they get a chance to talk about those books, to act them out, to dramatize them, and to make puppet plays about them, their proficiency in developing standard English speech is doubled in less than a year. All children who do more than just listen to a story increase their language power, but children from poor homes do significantly better. So once again the power of literature to ignite the child's learning is clearly demonstrated. The time to start? Well, if not at home, then in preschool classes and certainly in kindergarten. All children improve their language skills, and while they do it they are learning to love books.

school at home

when they learn too young

We need not swallow some of the educational gobbledygook dished up by those who think that three-year-olds need to go to school to learn skills. There are too many who feel that this idea will eventually sweep the country despite evidence to the contrary. Is there an alternative to the mass shipment of babes in arms to the impersonality of corner schools? I think so. The "school in the home" is a great idea that has been well tested. What is it? Simply put, it is the effort of professionals to go into the homes of people whose education and background have not prepared them for the complicated task of giving children the rich background of experience they need to learn and grow well. And what of the millions of mothers who are working or want to work? We need to care for their children, using persons who are more interested in warmth, continuity of affection, and dedication to the emotional needs of children than they are in "socking it to them" with arithmetic and spiritless reading from programmed texts. Let's not exploit intelligence.

The glamour of early childhood education has captivated the American imagination so that it seems that ill-advised people will swallow it hook, line, and sinker. They will rue the day as they breed a generation of knowledge-gulpers. Let me cite specific studies indicating the dangers of too early emphasis on formal learning. A psychologist for the American Educational Research Association found that children who began reading at seven, as opposed to a similar group who started at six, were in two years equal to the early beginning group. In seventh grade the late starters were ahead of the early ones. Margaret Gott in California compared kindergarten children who were enrolled early with those enrolled at a later age. After six grades of schooling, the younger children were behind the older ones, except in one instance. Inez King in Tennessee studied and compared fifty-four children who were under six when they started school with fifty children who started after six. Same results. In Michigan psychologists selected mature children to start school before five. After fourteen years one-fourth of the select group were below average.

three-year-old fish

early child care

28 I can't figure out what it is that makes Americans so wild about the idea of teaching people things they needn't learn so early in life. Witness the advertising campaign of a reading gimmick that says that you ought to teach your infant to read, that your infant, in fact, wants to learn and needs to learn to read. Then again we have leagues that are designed to make seven-year-olds act, play, and look like the Green Bay Packers and the Mets. Have you heard of the current craze over teaching infants to swim? Well, it is not impossible, but consider the dangers. The American Academy of Pediatrics recently condemned the idea, not because it is not possible, but because "under threes" can't really comprehend safety rules. In addition, they are unnecessarily exposed to intestinal viruses that being at home would guard against. Pools carry viruses for upper respiratory infection, and other potentially dangerous microorganisms can cause different diseases to which infants should not be unduly exposed. What you get out of teaching a three-year-old or younger to swim is very little indeed compared to the negative aspects.

Lest readers think I am on some bandwagon against preschool education, let me assure them that I grind no axes for any ideology. I am a reporter who tells it like it is, and let the intellectual chips fall where they may. Eighteen months ago in the Soviet magazine *Novy Mir* (*New World*), which is a state-owned publication, a Soviet mother raised the thorny issue of early child-care centers in Russia. Here are some facts: Nearly 80 percent of Soviet women between the ages of twenty and fifty-five hold jobs outside their homes. Obviously, most of the child care, once relegated to the nuclear family, must now be assumed by the state. Communal child rearing is designed there to encourage personality formation, which is in rigid conformity with collectivist ideology. In a nutshell, there is widespread dissatisfaction in Russia with this system. In America, advocates of early childhood education are not to be equated with collectivists. In most cases they are concerned, dedicated Americans, who want to make life better for children. Let them be aware, however, of dangers.

the physiology of early learning

educating preschool teachers

There are no special advantages in starting school early from an educational point of view. There are dangers to the developing child and his brain and nerves resulting from undue stress caused by too early emphasis on learning the basic skills. Paul Yakovlev of Harvard tells us that the nerve fibers between the thalamus and the cortex are not fully insulated before the age of seven. Also, between the ages of seven and ten the cerebral brain paths between brain lobes are not fully developed. This indicates that readiness for certain types of thinking necessary for reading and reasoning skills isn't there as early as hoped. Luella Cole observed that the lack of eye maturity before age eight can place undue stress on too early attempts to teach reading. Hilgartner, a Texas ophthalmologist, offers evidence that there is eye damage if reading is started too early. The work of Jean Piaget, the Swiss psychologist, indicates that until at least eight, full reasoning powers are simply not there. All of this adds up to caution when we push for too early schooling.

I have wailed loudly about the fact that when a national system of comprehensive day-care centers is a reality, there will be a shortage of the kinds of people needed to give the right kind of care to preschool-age children. Although the bill was vetoed by President Nixon, it seems a sure thing that it will come to pass sooner or later and probably sooner than we expect. My complaint has been that it takes warm and knowledgeable people to give young children the care that will help them to become emotionally reliable adults. We haven't mass produced that type of person yet, for the public schools and colleges of education throughout this land have just been ordered to cut back the number of eligibles for teacher training by 25 percent because of the shortage of jobs. We will rue this order, because we will be without the professional leadership needed to train the thousands of non-college people who will eventually have to do most of the day-care work. These child development associates will need to be taught some of the basics of child development, and who will do it? When we can see the wave of the future, we ought to prepare to meet it. As Pogo once said, "We have met the enemy, and he is us."

smart babies, smart adults?

the real cost of preschool education

For a very long time the scientific world believed that an infant's mental ability was a very accurate predictor of what his intelligence would be like when he grew up. Research at the Fels Institute in Ohio corroborates evidence that this view of infant intelligence is not accurate. The tests performed on infants may be accurate indicators of their present state of intelligence, but they are inaccurate predictors of future mental operational levels. The notion that intelligence is an unchanging characteristic is not sound. A smart baby will not inevitably grow into a smart adult. I have frequently had parents call and tell me about the remarkable mental development of their two-year-old. I do not doubt their optimism, but I do try to warn them that frantic efforts to predict the child's future accomplishments are wasteful. The strongest influences upon a child, influences that will affect his later intelligence, are the attention, approval, and involvement he has with concerned adults. A brilliant infant can retrogress if he does not continue to receive these vital lifelines as he grows.

There is no doubt but what the modern generation will be clamoring for day-care centers and mighty soon. In my own state our governor recently pressed for preschool education before a congressional committee. Neither parties are wrong or to be faulted for their zeal. I simply wish to reiterate what I have said over and over. If this generation learns *not* to care for its children, then it will create centers to dump them in. If women are to be liberated only to pawn their children off on some faceless, amorphous society, which will undoubtedly want to fill the "little jars" full of arithmetic and science, then we had all better hold our heads and weep. Children don't have Kate Millets or Jane Fondas to do their fighting for them, and so we may liberate our women and imprison our children. There's plenty the schools need now to humanize the children they teach. I fear that no tax dollars will support even more costly preschool education, especially if it's the kind that will really do more than baby-sit, and that's what is needed.

threatened children

autistic children

It is a valid psychological principle that a person being threatened can pay attention to nothing but that which threatens him. His capacity to perceive is narrowed to the object of threat. In rearing children, we want to widen their perceptions, not narrow them. Thus we need to provide many conditions that are not threatening. The difference between challenge and threat is in how the learner, in this case the child, views his world. A child who lives in a situation in which all exploration is viewed as a threat to his secure world is a threatened child. When he sees a task as a challenge that will improve him, he is not threatened but activated. A task worthy of all adults is to present tasks to children that challenge and do not threaten. Threat produces anxiety, which in turn causes aggression. Aggression produces frustration and hostility. Threatening situations cause children to curl up and retreat into safer worlds where their attention is wholly directed toward their survival, and that makes a pretty mean kid.

There is more to life than the oyster knows. There is more to life than intake and defense. Too often folks behave as if all there is to know as a human is how to protect one's self and how to eat. Babies need much more care than oysters. They need more than food and dryness. Autistic children are those who, like the oyster, rarely open up, and who just occupy space and time. Most major cities have wards in hospitals where many of these children languish. Among the reasons behind their stolid silence is that some of their earliest childhood experiences were so painful, so filled with hostility and grimness, that they decided somewhere along the line to clam up and renounce the world. They looked out on a hostile world and decided to have none of it. These infants seldom live very long. Humans need more than the barest rudiments of animal existence. They need all the warmth, affection, and attention that can be supplied. No machines can do this, no electrical wizardry can replace even an illiterate parent who cares enough to love.

causes of autism

32 I was recently accused of perpetuating the old-fashioned notion that autistic children develop from the effects of cold, unaffectionate parents. If I gave the impression that this is the *sole* cause of this problem in children, I am happy to correct that. Autistic children are most often nonspeaking, emotionally handicapped youngsters who often appear to be quite normal. They seem in many ways to have wrapped themselves up in a personal blanket of silence. There are other theories of the cause of autism that some claim are *indisputable;* others aver that they are *possible.* One of these is the genetic component, of which little is known. Other possibilities are neurological and biochemical bases for this disturbance that result in bizarre behavior, withdrawal, and personality disorganization. Mom and Dad have borne the brunt of society's accusation that they were inadequate. It is not all that simple, and I am willing to stand corrected if I ever left the impression that this type of parent is the *only* cause of autism.

hyperactive children

The hyperactive child has one of the most difficult kinds of behavioral disorders to live with because he does not provide any of the emotional satisfactions to his parents that other children do. As a result, this child often becomes the target of his parents' abuse. At about three months of age most babies start to settle into the family routine. Frequently the hyperactive child can be identified as early as the fourth month because he will not settle into any routine. He reacts erratically to the family; he is intensely disruptive to everyone and everything around him. Such a child is hard to love. In fact, his parents become so upset that in many cases he is rejected as being an impossible child, thus triggering guilt and shame in his parents who would like to love him but cannot. Whenever a parent must force himself to love a child, the strain in the relationship tends to produce a chain reaction of tension and disgust. It is advised that once parents and their pediatricians are able to identify this hyperactivity, the mere knowledge can help the parents to cope with their own emotions.

mongoloid children

preschool for the handicapped

Medical science still doesn't really understand why mongoloid infants have an Oriental appearance. Over 100 years ago, Dr. John Langdon Down described this form of mental retardation and thought that mongolism proved an ancient link between the Caucasian and Oriental races. We are certain that these children are not throwbacks to a more primitive race of man. We do know that geneticists have found an extra chromosome inside the cell nucleus. Where normal individuals have forty-six chromosomes, mongoloid children have forty-seven. Why that forty-seventh chromosome causes a child to have a skin fold at the corner of the eye, a broad nose, a protruding tongue, a single crease running the breadth of his palm, and an I.Q. of thirty, no one knows. Most mongoloid infants survive birth and grow up somewhat overly receptive to infection. Many are born with serious heart and intestinal defects. Modern surgery can correct most of these. The heart-rending question often is, should physicians operate to save the life of a child destined to lead a retarded existence?

The world is so full of unhappy things— drugs in the schools, child abuse, teenage crime, etc.—that it becomes a rare pleasure to report to you about some of the activities in behalf of children that often go unheralded. In St. Agnes Hospital in White Plains, New York, there is a preschool program for severely handicapped children. Recently there was a graduation during which time thirteen children received diplomas with Winnie-the-Pooh emblazoned on them, indicating that they were ready for further schooling. Some of the children had only learned to walk, some only to sit up, but each of these was a milestone in the life of the child. Multiply handicapped children are, during their infancy, often relegated to the scrap heap of humanity because they can't do what most others can. These scrap heap children go to school twelve months of the year, five days a week, and they learn to succeed at things they always failed at. The fact of the matter is, with care, instruction, perseverence, and love, any child can be brought from even a serious present state to some improvement.

parents of handicapped children

to drug or not to...

34 I was interested to learn that there are more divorces and separations during a handicapped child's second year of life than at any other time. In the first year children are quite helpless, and so it isn't until the handicapped child is able to strike out for himself that the shock of having a handicapped child registers on the parents. The normal and natural reaction is intense guilt feelings and then feelings of rejection, not only for the child but for one another. This psychological revulsion, a normal reaction, often needs to be suffered through with some psychological support from wise and humane professionals. Both of these feelings are sufficient to drive couples apart under the best of circumstances. If the handicap is discovered early and parents are counseled about how to relate to the child and each other, there is usually enough joy derived from the experience to outweigh the hostile feelings. Running from doctor to doctor is a frequent escape. Getting down to work at the problem is the only answer.

Recently several states have banned the use of amphetamines in the treatment of certain types of medical problems. Since they are addictive, these drugs produce a dependency that is often worse than the effects of the disease they have been used to eliminate. For example, in hyperkinetic children, or those who are severely overactive (perhaps you have seen the child who never seems to stop tearing things up or disrupting orderly situations), amphetamines have long been used to slow the child down. After he is slowed down a bit, his family and others can tolerate him so that he does not find himself rejected and cast out by the society that surrounds him. Yet he is in every sense of the word drugged. The evil of letting a child continue to become the object of scorn of all who live near or with him is self-apparent. The hyperkinetic child soon becomes a very severely disturbed personality and everyone suffers. To drug or not to drug is indeed a serious dilemma.

children's germs

kids nibbling plants

Believe it or not, except for emotional illness, 95 percent of children's diseases are contagious. In other words, children cannot catch any disease unless they are exposed to the germ. Man has had this priceless knowledge for nearly 100 years. Many childhood diseases come from dirty hands; some these include boils, sties, impetigo, staph pneumonia, dysentery, typhoid, and strep throats. Diseases among any group of children could be cut significantly if parents of the children would be particularly careful about hand washing. Some of the hand-washing rules are: wash well above the hand, nearly halfway to the elbow; use soap; and dry with paper towels. A towel, incidentally, is a real breeding ground for germs. It is used too often, it is always damp, and thus it cultivates the growth of bacteria. Towels should be taboo even though using paper hurts. In our house all children use nailbrushes, because clean hands without clean nails are self-defeating. So don't threaten, cajole, or scream. Just wash your hands perfectly, and your kids will follow the leader.

In the summer season of growing, I feel it important to report upon the research done at the Creighton University School of Medicine in Omaha, Nebraska. We see in our nation today a great and exciting movement that is returning people to nature. This back-to-basics movement means that more and more families are planting and growing more, and this means that wherever this takes place, at home or in the backyard, children below school age are more and more likely to nibble on plants and leaves. More than 500 species common in the U.S. are poisonous to humans. Poinsettias when chewed or eaten cause convulsions; iris, azaleas, rhododendron, and English holly all cause severe reactions in children. For example, if a child eats twenty to thirty berries from English holly, it will probably mean death or violent vomiting and diarrhea. Three popular houseplants —philodendron, dieffenbachia, and caladium—produce swelling of mouth and throat tissues when sampled. Unlike other poisons ingested that tend to cause immediate reactions, plants that are chewed may take twenty-four hours to have an effect. Watch the kids and their nibbling.

lead poisoning

measles and children

Dangers exist in old buildings where the paint is peeling and where little children often are seen chewing on the paint. After some period of time the children get lead poisoning, which is fatal. Recently a physician has advocated the enriching of whole milk with iron; this, he feels, would prevent lead poisoning. If you are having difficulty relating paint to enriched milk, let me try to clarify for you. You may recall that years ago, before the advent of calcium lactate pills, women who had just given birth used to be observed picking at the walls in their hospital rooms. Well, just after birth the body craves calcium, and one of the ingredients of plaster walls is, of course, calcium carbonate. So, too, children have a craving, for many of these children only get milk and not the other foods necessary to supply the iron they need. Thus this craving translates itself unconsciously into the nibbling at inedible substances known as pica. And that is how it happened that there were 452 cases of lead poisoning in New York City last year.

There are only seventeen states that make the immunization of children against measles mandatory. In my opinion this is frightening when you consider the awesomeness of the statistics about measles. One out of every fifteen children who contract measles will develop an immediate, serious complication. One out of every two children who contract measles will suffer a minor and subtle brain involvement. One out of two will, for as long as a year after recovery, be in poor health and require 400 percent more medical care than kids who never had the measles. It is a fact that half of the children who catch the measles develop an abnormal encephalogram or brain recording. Although this clears up in ten days, there are cases where there is permanent brain damage as long as a year after the encephalogram returns to normal. When the test scores of children who have had the measles are compared with those who have never had the disease, there is also evidence that reading readiness is retarded. Measles is serious business for children. What is your state doing?

doctors and drugs

allergies and surgery

In the fond hope that mothers might not find their pediatricians at fault for not prescribing medicine, I report to you today that in the considered opinion of many medical authorities, we over-medicate both young and old. When it comes to health, we are an anxiety-ridden nation. Most of the things that happen to children, even those which cause fever, need very rarely to be treated with life-saving drugs, which are too often wasted on the young. The best physician is the one who knows when to do nothing. You do not pay your physician for what he prescribes but rather for what he can tell you needs not to be done. His experience allows him to judge just when a medication is in order, and when he says it isn't, he is not neglecting his duty. Mothers often demand action from physicians, and too many gladly oblige in order that their lives will seem significant. When your doctor says, "Do nothing," he is telling you some very important information. Don't pressure him for drugs when nature has a wisdom of its own.

Allergies are a common ailment among children. They can be serious. Too often surgeons overlook asking parents about the allergenic condition of each child they plan to operate on. Parents, fearful of injecting their own feelings and observations into the medical scene, are afraid of telling the almighty surgeon anything. Allergies are not just those irritating conditions that develop during special seasons or after eating certain foods. Much allergy is highly related to one's emotional condition. A child about to undergo surgery frequently has severe trauma, deep anxieties, and fears about what is to become of him. At this time a hyperallergenic reaction is likely to be triggered, causing the same kinds of irritations to the skin and lungs as if there were a direct cause such as food present. Dr. Claude Frazier, in his volume *Surgery and the Allergic Patient*, cautions that lung functions must be done on a child who has asthma, and if a child has been on steroids before surgery, he probably should receive them before, during, and after surgery too. Physicians must know what it is the child is allergic to and what drugs have triggered attacks so that postoperative complications will not ensue.

leukemia

children in hospitals

38 There is both good news and bad on the medical front in the world of childhood. The good was reported at the Thirteenth Annual Seminar for Science Writers sponsored by the American Cancer Society. There Dr. Carl Baker reported that childhood leukemia may now be properly included among the few cancers that may be considered curable. Ninety-five percent of children with leukemia can be made free of the signs and symptoms of the disease. More than 74 percent of children with leukemia are alive two years after diagnosis. Before the advent of drug therapy, 70 percent were dead two months after diagnosis and nearly all at three to four months after diagnosis. I can't think of any better news. On the negative side, the U.S. Center for Disease Control reported last year that there has been a terrible lag in immunizations of children. Measles is out of control, diphtheria is at its highest incidence in nearly a decade, and we are on the verge of polio epidemics. Public complacency over immunization is the cause. Immunization is a great achievement, but without being put to use it has little effect.

When a child is hospitalized, the deepest hurts he suffers have nothing to do with the severity of his surgery or the pricks of needles. It is his sense of abandonment and helplessness that is excruciating. In both London and Sweden there are hospitals that understand well what is meant by treating the whole child. It is not just his illness alone that must be treated; it is the depressing experience of being cut off from familiar faces of mother and father that really hurts — especially where he is hospitalized for infectious diseases and may not see or communicate with others of his family and friends. And so, two hospitals have installed intramural phones so that hospitalized children can communicate freely with anyone in the hospital. In Sweden a hospital for children has twenty-four-hour visiting hours, hotel apartments for parents, a swimming pool, theater, sauna, and indoor and outdoor play areas for whoever can use them. There is even a four-room school for children well enough to study. That's taking the horror out of hospitalization.

shyness in the hospital

child abuse

As in everything in the world of science and fiction, there are myths that have developed because of the not very astute observations of ordinary folk. Some myths develop because people would rather believe myths than facts. And finally, some myths develop because people really think they observe certain phenomena. For years we thought that the majority of children beaten by their parents and classified as child-abuse cases were unwanted children. There is some startling evidence from the medical center at the University of Southern California that the majority of children beaten by their parents are the result of planned pregnancies. Since the advent of the birth control pill, child beating has gone up threefold. Sixty percent of the people who beat their babies are poverty-stricken, 40 percent are "comfortably fixed," and nine percent have higher education. The home is usually, however, a strict home. Finally, those who abuse their children tend to show they were abused as children themselves.

We know of a little lad who is acutely ill with some kind of leukemia. Since he is only three and has spent more than one-third of his life under medical care, he has developed a certain shyness toward hospital personnel; and in their well-meaning attempt to bring him out of his shell of fear and wonderment, nurses, aides, and physicians will approach him as he hangs his little head and exclaim about the fact that little John won't say anything at all to them. He has a lot to say at home, but at the hospital he crawls inside of himself and hides. The professionals who deal with him do love him, but they don't realize that shaming him by alluding to his muteness will never break open his silence. They simply ought to talk to him warmly and normally and never make reference to his silence, which he comes by quite naturally. By paying little attention to his quiet behavior, they will more likely open him up.

more on child abuse

teaching them to ride

40 The research literature concerned with adults who have uncontrollable urges to beat up their children is both intensely disturbing and shocking. Parents who have these horrible urges can be stopped if they have some sort of instant mothering available to them. Just at that moment of crisis, it is possible now in Denver and in Great Britain to call a number and have a comforting mother-type person come swiftly to the home of the enraged parent and give comfort to the person who is losing control. These nonprofessionals are people who, though untrained academically, are loving mother and father figures themselves. Dr. Henry Kempe, the man who originated the term "battered child syndrome," has been training mothering aides who are willing, for one-twentieth the price of a psychiatrist, to leave their own homes at a moment's notice to mother a parent who is losing control. Emotional deprivation in childhood is still the most common reason for a parent's becoming an abuser of his own children.

No father easily forgets the pleasure of seeing his child's eyes sparkle as he approaches the Christmas tree and sees the dream of childhood—a two-wheel bike of his own. And no father easily forgets the fatigue and concern he goes through as he takes the child and the new bike into the streets on Christmas day, despite snow and storm, to give junior his first ride. But if junior has never learned to ride, things aren't always as pleasant as they were when the vehicle lay shining beneath the tree, magnificent in its glitter but destined to dormancy until the owner learns to ride. So, here are some tips for dad on teaching junior to master the vehicle. First make sure the seat is low enough for the child's feet to touch the ground. Let him warm up by straddling the seat and walking the bike; then have him coast down a mild slope with feet off the ground. On level ground, hold the bike firmly until the child gets the feel of pedaling. Use a lawn on which he can practice circling until his balance is sure. Patience and love will carry the day. Try it. You'll like it.

children in public

I'd like to try to answer some commonly asked questions about disciplining children. Parents often wonder why it is that while at home their children respond quite well to instructions, are courteous, and are really quite delightful, but when the family is in a public place such as a theater lobby, an airline terminal, or a department store—suddenly all of the previous good behavior disappears. The parent is usually at a loss for what to do. Two or three things are worth looking at for a minute. If the child really behaves reasonably at home but not in public, then the parent needs to at once take him by the arm and march him out; then a good tongue-lashing needs to be applied. If this doesn't work, a good talk and a swift spank on the bottom, in public, won't hurt. It is also possible that if this two-sided behavior is too evident, the behavior at home has been too controlling and hasn't really been internalized. Children need to know that the rules of behavior apply everywhere.

young children in cars

While driving toward the University of Utah the other day, I looked across the street into a car driven by a pretty mother in her late twenties. She was just leaning over the driver's seat, reaching with her arm toward a toddler in a car seat who was throwing plastic foam balls at the windshield. As she reached over to her right, her car veered and nearly scraped a passing vehicle. And so Lady Luck intervened and nothing happened, but too many accidents are caused by babies and toddlers who, not knowing the consequences of their childish fun, are victims of many accidents each year. In a car, adult power must be absolute, and discipline is not a matter of simply leaning over or down. When a child misbehaves in a car, he is unwittingly being distracting, and he must never be dealt with by the driver while the car is in motion. It is imperative that you do not attempt to smack him or restrain him until you have pulled over and completely stopped. Settle the matter firmly then and there, and then drive on.

who shouldn't baby-sit?

pets and kids

 Two doctors recently studied the murders of five infants by children two and a half to eight years of age. Five babies, all between seven and eight months of age, were killed by older children who were not their siblings. My reading of this study indicates that it is very risky to leave very young children, those under the age of a year, with any children who aren't at least eleven or older. Small children cannot cope with some of the crying and temper behaviors of infants under a year. The combination of jealousy, a child's lack of understanding of his own strength, and the infant's weakness is enough to lead to an "accidentally on purpose" tragedy. Note that it is not really the older child's wish to kill; it is simply that the older child doesn't have full cognition of the fact that the younger child's life is important. A child's motives for beating a baby may be generalized hostility toward his own infant sibling who represents a threat, jealousy, or a curious contempt for the babyish behavior of the younger child.

The words of Kathleen Szasz, as she discusses the influence of pets upon children, reveal a most accurate indictment of our family life. She says, "In America children depend on pets for the sense of security they can't get from overpermissive parents. The pet is always there. It does not go to work or, in the evening, to social functions like Daddy, or to the psychoanalyst and morning coffee and gossip parties like Mommy. It does not come late at night, exhausted, and often slightly drunk; it does not quarrel and, most important of all, does not divorce. Children give love freely, and without reservation, and their pets respond. When did a dog lose his temper and stalk out of the house? When did a puppy ever say one thing and do another?" Poor analogy, perhaps, but it makes the point that a little less intellect and a little more commitment never hurt anyone's children.

one bed for all

temper, temper

Many parents face the thorny problem of whether to allow their children to share their bed either regularly or on occasion. There isn't a great deal of scientific evidence one way or the other. It seems to me that common sense, so often uncommon, suggests that children usually prefer to sleep alone unless they are frightened and need comfort and reassurance. Children's dreams and fears are, like those of adults, very real and very fearful. There is no harm I can see that will accrue to a child who, upon first asking to sleep with his parents, is allowed to. Usually a week or less of this helps fears subside, and junior goes back to his own bed. In many parts of the world one-bed families are the rule, and no one seems to be able to identify any serious consequences to the child's psyche. It appears that it simply is not a western custom to promote bed sharing in families. Apparently much of this is related to the western idea of allowing privacy for the nocturnal activities of parents. Far be it from me to deride the custom. I can only indicate that abnormal child development doesn't start because of bed sharing.

How does a child get his way when he knows that if he asks he will be refused? The temper tantrum is the usual mechanism, and it is a powerful weapon because it strikes a cold fear in the hearts of mothers, especially if it happens with their first child. The tantrum is not only a response to an expected refusal, however; it is also rage and anger that are not able to be voiced because the child does not have sufficient vocabulary at his command. An adult in anger can vent his spleen by cussing, or kicking, or reading the riot act, which means to say plenty. The toddler who has a tantrum cannot do this. For one thing, he has learned that he cannot talk back to his mother. He has been prohibited this verbal ventilation by the standards of his family. I am not saying that this should not be the case; I am simply explaining that tantrums result from verbal inadequacy when there is anger and frustration. The best way to handle a tantrum— in the words of a popular song— is to let it be and it will run its course. Then follow it with love and a verbal explanation of why you said no.

children as rivals   predicting antisocial adults

44

If you have ever felt that your children never stop fighting at home, and I am sure that if you have a few at home you've experienced this, then you'll be happy to know that even though it is enough to drive you mad, it is normal, natural, and in many ways beneficial to the growth and development of your children. There are many frustrations in the child's life. There are many in adult lives too. Adults can work off their aggression in many ways, but children cannot revolt against their parents, and so they often take out their aggression on their siblings. Sibling rivalry is a sort of competition between children, and in moderate amounts it enhances a child's self-esteem, especially if it is an older child making the younger one pay for his youth. What I am trying to say is that if parents keep a sharp eye out for the kinds of things that are happening between their children, they can learn when to intervene and when to let rivalry go on in the interests of normal growth and development of the family. Competition in moderation is constructive and can stimulate achievement.

There is some danger that the findings reported here may be overinterpreted. Listen carefully. A University of Texas research team has linked four childhood behavior patterns with violent, antisocial behavior in adulthood. Many who grow up to commit murder, rape, assault and armed robbery exhibited *all* of these behaviors in their childhood. First, chronic, excessive fighting that really hurts other children. Second, multiple school problems, including truancy, poor grades, lack of self-confidence. Third, severe temper tantrums that persist beyond the preschool years, hurt others, and destroy property. Finally, a chronic inability to make and keep friends and a compulsion to be alone. All of these problems are exhibited by most children. It is *only* when all four appear excessively in one child and when they occur at inappropriate ages that we have what is known as a "constellation of behaviors." A child who shows a persistence and a continuation of these symptoms is indicating that something is seriously wrong. While not sure predictors, they indicate a greater proneness to violent behavior.

who's gifted

our child's differences

What parent doesn't like to feel that he has produced a gifted child? Many of the calls I receive are from parents who are elated over the prospect, and most want to know how they can tell if their child is gifted. The answer is that only about 2 percent of the population has such an offspring, and there are ways of determining this. The greatly gifted child will accomplish nearly every developmental phase, such as walking, talking, toilet training, and playing on his own, years ahead of every other child you've known or heard about. By years ahead I mean very much earlier than others. Obviously, an early talker cannot physically talk years ahead of anyone, but if he starts to talk at eleven or twelve months instead of the usual seventeen to twenty months, he may be gifted. To jump years ahead, the truly gifted child will, by the time he is eleven or twelve, have the unusual capacity to seem as if he has a very definite life plan. He is able to determine and guide most of his activities in such an extraordinary way that he stands head and shoulders above anyone you have ever heard of before.

Though most people feel that children grow differently, learn differently, and are the products of different cultural and ethnic patterns, we overstress the idea that they should weigh so much, be so tall, be developed like the other children. We are overly concerned that they learn to read at five or six and now, with the modern push for the abolition of childhood through hard work and study, to read at three. We are also perturbed when there is slow or early physical growth. The concept of the neighborhood oddball is still with us, and we "tut-tut" when our children do not meet the standards of the neighborhood or the classroom. What do we really believe? Almost everything about children is measured against some standard. Perhaps we sincerely want our children to come out of fluted molds. Since society talks from both sides of its mouth, children soon learn when they don't fit preconceived patterns. It doesn't take a child long to catch on to the idea that his differences are a source of concern, not a source of delight.

no fair generalization about children

46 Like the ancients who sought for the fountain of youth, parents today are continually searching for the magic formula for rearing children successfully. Once upon a time that formula was discipline—spare the rod; spoil the child. Later it was permissiveness; and still later, even that enlightened idea was frowned upon. No, I am not proposing any new catchall formula, just reminding you that every shred of research about children indicates that their personality differences are so pronounced that each needs to be governed by that which works best for him. Drs. Chess and Thomas in their book *Your Child Is a Person* indicate that their studies show 40 percent of babies to be easy to rear, 10 percent to be difficult, with 15 percent described as slow to warm up. The remaining 35 percent studied had a mixture of temperaments. Don't make any generalizations about children—that is the only safe generalization.

schools and the children they teach

In recent conversations, friends who are members of the psychiatric community estimated that better than 75 percent of the children they see who are having problems at home have a school-based difficulty. In our present society, where school starts for many children at the age of six and seven and continues for at least twelve years, it may fairly be said that the school is one of the major influences on a child's life. A telephone call just the other day makes the above statements even more vivid.

A mother, in desperation, reported that her two-year-old daughter (now nearly three) was going to nursery school and enjoying it rather well. Suddenly, about a week ago, just three or four days prior to the father's leaving to fulfill his assignment in the Air National Guard, the child reacted violently to going to nursery school. She had a temper tantrum, cried endlessly, threw up, refused to go to school, and in general, was exceedingly upset. The other facts of the case are in and of themselves interesting: this child is a stepchild to the mother and only recently joined the mother and her new husband after being with her original mother for the past year and a half or more.

While it is sufficient to guess at this point that this child suffered severe trauma in the year and a half separation from her father, it is, nonetheless, clear that the preschool situation that was necessary because of the stepmother's going to work was, if not the cause, at least the catalyst to the child's upset. So, while a moment ago we stated that American children are subjected to twelve years of schooling through the secondary school years, we may now add to this the two to three years of school many children get as they have preschool experiences.

Preschool experiences are here to stay, it seems, and in the immediate future it does not seem likely that compulsory education will be done away with. Therefore, with schooling being such a major part of a child's emotional, intellectual, and social experience, it is urgent that we pay attention to the various facets of the school experience that impinge upon the child's life.

This section will relate most specifically to the child in the elementary school: the child between ages six and twelve, the schools that he attends, and the things in his life that influence him most in these years. Therefore, the reader should be prepared to encounter my comments about not only the schools and the children in them, their teachers, and their curriculum, but also nearly every kind of happening that is relevant to the life of children between the ages of six and twelve, from art in the schools, to vandalism, to the little league, sex differences, lying, homosexuality, I.Q., and the child's family.

These are the years when a youngster either develops a sense of industry, meaning that he considers himself to be able and achieving, or a sense of inferiority, in which he considers himself to be unable to learn, to progress, and to become.

This six- or seven-year period of time helps determine greatly if the child will be able to meet the adolescent identity crisis with courage and confidence or with trepidation. These so-called "middle years," or what Freud called the period of psychosexual latency (though there is abundant evidence that the latency Freud talked about has been reawakened like some sleeping giant), are years in which the child's school experiences either contribute to his total feeling of competency or detract from it, thus causing him to build himself or to feel incompetent and deficient, and thus inferior.

The reader might find it interesting at this point to consider the hypothesis that the current push in the country for equality of education is one that has focused primarily on the elementary school years. The reasons for this are many, but one that is not often discussed is the fact that the kinds of things that are occurring in this developmental period of childhood—i.e., industry versus inferiority—may be closer to the heart of the matter than even those who are pushing for school equality may realize. It is entirely probable and possible that inferior schooling in the ages six through twelve may result in a lifelong handicap. If during this time in a child's life he does not develop a powerful sense of industry, he does not achieve in the academic fields, and he does not feel that he is a worthwhile, significant, and adequate individual, then we are probably sowing the seeds for his future to be dismal and under-achieving. America needs to be concerned about all of its children, and it will never do to have any large segment of the population feeling deficient, defeated, and eventually defiant.

It is also during these years that parents and families need to understand that at home, too, the child must feel that he is valued, needed, and integral to the success of the family. These middle years build upon the first six years, yet they may be a time of no progress if the first six years were grossly deficient. One of the powerful concepts developed by neo-Freudians and other psychologists is that one is not doomed irrevocably to failure by the deficiencies of any particular growth period. In other words, it is possible for a rich school experience to bring a child out of the doldrums that he may have suffered during the first six years of his life. Erikson's belief that in all of the periods of our lives we relive the developmental challenges of previous ones is a formulation I uphold. What seems perfectly clear to me is that the better and stronger all of the periods of our lives are, the easier it is for us to meet disappointment, difficulty, even disaster.

I am particularly convinced that the early school years (kindergarten to grades six or seven) are an indispensable part of the developmental cycle and that too much attention cannot be paid to choosing schools, teachers, and administrators who will consciously and deliberately enrich these years for the children. I see the teachers, the principals, the lunchroom helpers, the custodian, the nurse, and the visiting specialists as all being indispensable in creating a therapeutic

environment for middle graders. When this is accomplished or when it is the direction in which a school is going, it becomes evident in the progress of the children in the school. There is a purpose in their learning, there is spirit and drive in their activity, and there is an independence and flair that does not represent objection to the status quo but is a healthy response to it. I have often said that I smell the intellectual, emotional, and social atmosphere of a school as I go in the front door. It doesn't take long to discover if I have smelled inaccurately. The purposeful direction of the school that attempts to build accomplishment, that attempts to meet children where they are, that attempts to take them from where they are to where they ain't (this is known as the process of education) is easily detected.

It has been said that the only true education a child gets is from his mother. What he gets from school is information. What he gets from his mother and his home is refinement, culture, ethics, and morals. I believe this to be largely true; yet I am of the opinion that a great school is a place where the middle-years child may learn with direction yet with freedom. He may emulate adults who are fine human beings interested in his individual growth

the worth of a child

52 and development. He may learn to see himself as an achieving, competent, valued member of society. Should this not be the case, we had better close the doors of the school and spend public monies elsewhere.

The accountability that is everywhere being bandied about must not mean mere accountability for academic excellence. The years between six and twelve are far too important to be wasted only on reading, writing, and arithmetic. None of these studies have ever developed character. The true purpose of school is not simply to be accountable for the academic excellence of children. It is to be accountable for the developing human beings that come from a particular building, a particular faculty, and a particular philosophy endemic to the school district. Anything less than this shortchanges our youth.

A child in prayer once said, "I know I must be somebody, because God don't make no junk." The significance of this plea is that teachers and parents need to be reminded that nearly every child can learn something important to him, provided the adults in his life also believe he can learn and, what's more, provided they set to find the means to teach each child. By the time a child comes to school he wears an invisible price tag—the sum of the way he sees himself. The warmth of a teacher's understanding and confidence can increase that price tag without inflation. I have stressed the importance of teachers never giving up on a child until they find the particular combination that unlocks the secrets to each child's unique way of learning. Every child can and will learn. A child's plea that he is not junk is very real, and yet even in some very fine schools there are children returning home each night who have been untouched by their teacher's hands and heart. One of our very real problems is the fear we have of play—that somehow it is degrading and not academic. Play is the child's work and very necessary.

helping children inquire

the joy of discovery

No one can make you a certified science teacher in just one minute, and I don't pretend that I can. I think I can, however, help you realize the important contribution a parent can make to aiding a child in his quest for information about the world. It is generally agreed today that science instruction is more a process of inquiry than telling. You may recall that during your school days you probably had a book open to a page in your science text and you read about science. In your home you can easily create the inquiry approach by wondering with your children. For example, a spider is going up the wall. Your child sees it, points, and says, "Look!" You look and then go back to tidying the sink. What you should do is say, "I wonder what keeps it on the wall," or "How many legs has it?" or "Where do you think it is going?" Each of these inquiries on your part forces the child to think and inquire for himself. Every time you get the opportunity to activate thought and language in your child, you are increasing his I.Q. and his delight in the world around him.

When a group of playground designers decided to create a stimulating environment for children, they equipped a space with real playthings—a house, a rocket so children could play astronaut, an old two-seater plane, and they let it go at that. A child's playground needs to be more varied and energetic. Observations of children show that they learn about themselves and the world through their play. In play children test their mental and physical coordination. Thus, they don't need expensive stuff, but places and things to climb, to run over, to bend down to, to twist, to mold and shape, to dig. You can use your own backyard and design the kinds of things that will allow for this. But that's not all. Children need to test the nature of the world, and so they need new forms from wood and concrete. They need caves, streams, hills, grass, tunnels, a stage, perhaps an island, old shacks, ropes, tree houses, trees, grass, sand, even some fences. They also need ladders, igloos, wading pools, water channels, and a surfaced area for bikes and toys. Anything less is cheating them.

play and fantasy   children's play

54 When one of Albert Einstein's friends suggested to him that there seemed to be a connection between mathematics and writing fiction, Einstein replied, "When I examine myself and my methods of thought, I come to the conclusion that the gift of fantasy has meant more to me than my talent for absorbing positive knowledge." And there are still teachers who feel that they must not waste the time of their students with oral reading from the great masters of fantasy and fiction for children. Recent ideas about preschool experiences are okay provided they do not mean immediate emphasis on decoding words and numbers. This would put the child's nose to the grindstone early, and it could result in his growing up with a sharp nose but a flat head. There is nothing wrong with the world of play and fantasy. Both are valuable, not to teach concepts surreptitiously, but for themselves. Play is for fun. So are games for fun. Shall we do away with the children's hour?

There are many newfangled words in use that really stand for the same old things we've been talking about for a long time. Let me give you a simple example: You've probably heard the term *reinforcement.* All it means is that in order to get done things that we wish to see happen, we reward the doer. Children learn by modeling; years ago we called it imitation. The cognitive structure of a school is what we once called the school's stress on thinking and reasoning. And so it goes. There are those who wish to do away with play in the name of some more appropriate gobbledygook that seems to be more relevant to the times. Children's play is important because it is on play that they test their perceptions of the world. Watch two children testing their assertiveness as they order one another around. At which point will one stop and give in to the other? At the point where their supposedly pointless play will teach them that they have overstepped their bounds. Sure it's play, but it teaches reality.

do schools make any difference?

what is educational?

The most talked-about book in education published this year is called *Inequality: A Reassessment of the Effect of Family and Schooling in America.* In a nutshell here's the argument. Americans have pursued the notion, say authors Christopher Jencks and Mary Jo Bane, that schools and schooling can solve our social ills. Equalizing the opportunity to fail or succeed does not change the chance that poor people will alter their status faster. Differences between schools, they argue, have very little effect on what happens to students after they graduate. Equalizing educational opportunity will not go far toward eliminating inequality. Desegregated schools do not produce markedly different scores for anyone, either blacks or whites. Even allocating resources disproportionately to schools whose students now do worse on tests would not improve these students' future prospects much. If schools don't make a difference to one's chances for success in life, then what does? Nothing but the serious reordering of our entire social structure, Jencks says, will have any effect. Well, that's one man's opinion. Watch out for the fireworks!

Not all experiences are educational. While I tend to applaud the exciting efforts of certain critics of our educational system, I also recognize that in a zest to turn out the old and sweep in the new, too many school people may equate aimlessness—every kind and manner of experience and change—as equivalent to progress. In order to be educational, an experience needs to be guided, conceptualized, planned, and relevant to the ongoing experiences of the group concerned. John Dewey once said, "All genuine education comes through experience." The debasement of this statement is what some overeager and undereducated folks might interpret it to mean, namely, that all experiences are genuinely educational. There is no real substitute for a well-conceived series of educational experiences with a reasonable structure. The demise of progressive education came about when children were heard to say as they entered school, "Do we have to do what we want to do today?"

a look at readiness

what is teaching?

It is a topsy-turvy world even in child growth and development. One day we believe that early deprivation of intellectual stimulation dooms a child to the academic scrapheap forever; the next we discover that it doesn't make too much difference. One day we are certain that early schooling makes a bright child; the next day we learn that early learning doesn't stick. One day it's feeding on demand; the next it is structured feeding. And so it goes. Until very recently we were fairly certain that a child's readiness to learn arithmetic and reading coincided with his entrance into school. Today we are fairly certain that the readiness to read and calculate occurs much later than we thought. In fact, it is probable that until most children reach nine or ten they can't handle with any ease the conceptual abilities that are needed in mathematics. Another finding is that children need more specific and precise instructions on how to do things than was thought previously. Substantial instructional assistance is what this help is now called, and it really means that what we have done in early child education is to fill the kids with rote learnings and little else.

Recently a friend said she was going to carefully check out her neighborhood public school so that she could be sure teachers there really were teaching the children. When I asked what her definition of teaching was, it seemed clear that she meant telling. Much of teaching, perhaps too much of it, is telling. I suggested she try to look at the teaching effectiveness of her school from another point of view. Suppose she were able to check the amount of time teachers spent at their desks not doing anything resembling interaction with children. I define interaction as saying or doing something to or with children. Teaching is not only telling; it is some of this. When a teacher is sitting down at his desk too much of any school day, and there are no children around him asking, discovering, wondering, then we may fairly conclude that he isn't teaching. Teaching is meddling with children, pointing the way, suggesting alternatives, encouraging, doing. When a teacher is separated from children by a desk or by a mind otherwise occupied, he isn't teaching.

teaching criteria   judging schools

While I was in California a while ago, I heard about a proposal that seeks to hold teachers accountable for the progress of their students. Teachers will be expected to define their objectives with each child and then to reach these objectives or be held very strictly accountable. In fact, I am told that the proposed bill specifically calls for periodic evaluation of teaching effectiveness, with the ever-present threat of being discharged from the system even if tenure has been previously granted. I like the idea of teachers setting goals for all their students so long as those goals are shared by the child. I don't think children are automobiles that can be tested as exactly as we'd like to believe. Indeed, whenever we really think that we can chart a person's learning as simply as we can his heartbeat, we will have achieved a millennial objective. Too many conditions make this plan an unfair hardship on those who teach the millions in schools who come from homes where it doesn't matter too much whether you learn or not. Too many children are all messed up emotionally long before school ever starts to insist that they too be taught with criteria. We all need to do better, not just teachers.

Schools are often hounded by their patrons because new changes such as open schools, affective education, schools without walls, and student-involvement schools do not produce either dramatic or even significant changes in the achievement scores of students. When a board of education sees no change in intellectual accomplishments, members tend to frown upon the new procedures and move in the direction of cutting funds from such programs. What is serious here is the fact that a new set of criteria for the evaluation of success in schooling is urgently needed. In the business world new change must result in increased profits, and whether this occurs or not is easily seen in any year-end report. But suppose there is a qualitative increase, perhaps in the emission control of a particular engine. The public too often is way behind the knowledge of qualitative improvement in products and for some time to come may continue to purchase an inferior product even though a far superior one is obtainable just around the corner. Schools aren't engines and can't be judged solely by test scores or sales.

afraid of school   all-year school

58 School phobia is a real emotional disease for certain children. In a school in which I am consulting, we have a ten-year-old boy who has had constant pains in the stomach through the day while he is at school, while as soon as he gets home he feels great. Then the next day the pains start all over again. The symptoms—nausea, vomiting, cramps—which all occur just before the school bus arrives and often from waking time on, are real and must be considered even if they disappear when the parent gives permission for the child to stay at home. School phobia cannot be pinpointed to a specific school cause but usually relates to the child's fear of keeping up and succeeding before peers and others. The fears are as real as real can be, even though it seems quite logical that there is no real need to be fearful. When a child is so incapacitated as to be unable to function in school, then this phobia or fear must be given professional help. The younger the child the easier the phobia is to cure, so parents and teachers need to be alert for suffering school phobics.

In Romeoville, Illinois, there is a year-round school. Their school calendar is called the "45-15" plan, and it works something like this: After every forty-five days of school, pupils are sent home for a vacation of fifteen school days. Here's how it all happened. When the school district reached its legal limit of bonding, no more schools could be built, so some way had to be found to keep the schools open more of the time to educate the burgeoning population. In other words, 25 percent of the students are always on vacation, thus allowing the other 75 percent a full school schedule. Not that there haven't been any changes in the life of the people. There certainly has. Little league baseball has died, and summer camping programs are withering. Other changes have been the cancellation of long vacations for children; shoplifting is a year-round thing; and baby-sitters who can stay up late are readily available.

dreams of school teaching the one

I think I'll have a pipe dream today, so sit back, relax, and dream along with me as I envision a more ideal school year than the one we traditionally have. Recently I described a school district where the children went to school for forty-five days and were on vacation for fifteen days. The upset in so many routines probably isn't worth it, but I do envision the taxpayer getting just a little bit more for his money, while the child gets just a little bit more learning. I have always said that "more of the same" is no bargain in our schools. But if we ever open the schools for real individualization of instruction, and if we ever come to believe that the arts and crafts and physical education are as valuable as anything else, and if we ever act as if we believe that music, mechanics, and cooking are vital to human growth and delight, we will start to look at our schools differently. I'd prefer to see some four-day weekends in school and a full nine-to-ten-month school year, with programs that are full of the good things in life.

When teachers learn together, school becomes very exciting. I am presently working with seventy teachers in a public elementary school where we have gathered nearly one hundred children and placed them in non-graded, interest-centered, individualized teaching situations. These seventy teachers have each been assigned one or two children with whom they work for a four-week period of time. Each child has his own teacher, and they are pretty thrilled about this one-to-one relationship. Each teacher is trying to get to know each child as a learner, and this isn't easy. Teachers, you see, are used to working with children in groups. In fact, they are most comfortable when the children have been grouped according to their ability. When you give a teacher a real child of his own, one for whom he can plan and arrange as he pleases, it presents a very distinct challenge. It is one thing to plan for many, a very different thing when you have just one to work with. School teaching is difficult. Most folks would just as soon be a plow mule, but mules do not glory in achievement, and humans must; so it's worth it.

ungrading schools

learning through teaching

60 I am presently involved in a school situation in which over 100 children are being taught in ungraded groups, where it really doesn't make any difference how tall or how old they are. Quite a few researchers today are much in favor of completely ungrading the elementary schools. Basically I think it is a good idea. My suggestion, however, due to the present uneasiness of parents and school people when it comes to mass change, would be to ungrade the first three grades so that during these earliest school years every child will learn without the stigma of failing or being behind the others. Learning disabilities become much more complicated the older we get, and our feelings about ourselves become more acute as we grow older and are more painfully aware of personal inadequacies. These 100 children we are working with now are ungraded, and I would defy anyone to guess precisely who is a third grader and who is a first grader. Incidentally, we have taken the middle road and ungraded grades one to three and as a separate unit grades four to six. Watching children help each other is fun for everyone.

We traditionally have children learning in competition with one another. That is, when we assign grades and put up excellent work for display, we are really pitting children *against* one another. In many schools around the nation we are now using children to help other children. What really happens is that the child, who is ostensibly helping another, is in reality learning, or relearning, or even overlearning, that which he needs mastery in. LTT, or learning through teaching, is nothing new. What is surprising is how few schools trust children enough to build the LTT idea into the school program. Rather than have children sitting passively about in the traditional reading circle waiting their turn, while eight or ten others blab their way through reading materials, a one-to-one relationship between a sixth grader and a third grader can make the most of the usual forty-minute reading time. If pupils play the teacher role often, then we are well on our way to what we dream of—the individualization of instruction.

open classrooms

class and caste in the schools

The specter of what has been called "open" classrooms in Great Britain looms upon the U.S. educational horizon. In England the concept has gained acceptance because it frees both pupils and teachers for more creative kinds of educational experiences. No fault here. In the United States caution needs to be exercised because it isn't all that easy to open up the children or the classrooms to the freedom of the British idea just by proclaiming the divinity of the notion. There are no predetermined lesson plans. The teacher is not at the head of the class. There is little domination by authority. There is no educational gospel, though there are many educational prophets in the land. Instant reform isn't easy. English children are better suited to new freedom because they are generally more disciplined. Principals in America are still viewed as "snoopervisors." Until all understand the new openness, we had better make haste slowly. Chaos has never been good for children and is more difficult to live under than dictatorship.

What makes for success in school? A white, affluent child whose father went to college has a better chance of succeeding in the public schools than other children. Conversely, big city children of poor, minority-group parents are most likely to score low on standardized tests, drop out of high school, and not go on to college. There is, then, a close parallel between your socioeconomic group and school success. In the past we have automatically concluded that our public school system, because it is public and requires no tuition other than taxes, opens the doors to achievement and success. This is not the case, and it never has been. Some children are programmed for failure from the start. One of the great tasks of the public schools is not in designing curriculum geared more and more to gadgets, but to really break through in the area of reaching all of the children despire class or caste. For too many, the schools only guarantee failure.

61

teaching reading

teachers and reading

 The quality of urban education is always subject to review and argument. The heart of the debate revolves about why some inner-city schools can and do teach their children to read while others don't. It has been especially heartening to me to discover what I have maintained for years. There is no magic formula, no one program that guarantees the difference. There are instead six factors that must be present in each school so that inner-city children will learn. They are (1) strong leadership in the form of teachers who are enthusiastic; (2) high expectations where children are not doomed to failure; (3) strong emphasis on reading, but not exclusive concern for the skills; (4) specialists in reading, so that instruction can be more individual; (5) the use of phonics in an important but not exclusive way; and (6) the individualization of instruction, which means more than just letting children work on their own level but rather continually responding to the precise needs of each child. Not simple, but possible.

If you think your schools have problems in teaching reading, take comfort from the fact that in New York City half the kids are above national norms and half below. New York decided to study those schools where more than half of the children scored above norms even though there was a vast majority of minority children—usually blacks and Puerto Ricans —who tend to depress a school's reading scores. We'll take Public School 91 as an example of an achieving school; it is 80 percent black and 9 percent Puerto Rican. First, reading is really stressed. It is every teacher's preoccupation. Most of the teaching of reading is on a small-group or individual basis. The principal follows every child's progress closely. He doesn't just collect lunch monies. No one reading program is used. The whole arsenal of reading materials finds its way into every class. The real key is not the use of any particular reader or program, but the teacher who is committed to reading improvement. Though home environment is a real factor, it can be overcome at least temporarily.

american reading skills

when to start teaching reading

Sometimes troublemakers, though they stir the waters and get folks really up-tight, do make waves that eventually have a positive effect upon society's waters. And so when a national study of the reading skills of 100,000 children and young people was conducted, the results were very promising. Let me hit the highlights for you. In general all age groups did better than any other studies have heretofore indicated. For example, there were 500 test exercises, and it was expected that only 50 percent would be successfully answered. Instead 70 percent were correctly answered. All groups did best on exercises testing the functional aspects of reading, such as reading signs, labels, directions, newspapers, and telephone listings. Unfortunately scores were lower where the ability to interpret and to discriminate between fact and fiction was concerned. More than 50 percent of nine- and thirteen-year-olds were unable to isolate the main ideas of test paragraphs. Things are not all dark in reading, but the "trouble-makers" of the sixties should get some credit.

My colleague, Malcolm Douglas from Claremont College, California, has in a rather unique way put the question of when to teach reading and how much reading to teach to children. He indicates that there is very little data to show that teaching the subject matter of reading leads to any proficiency. He feels, and I agree with him, that the skills of reading can be taught to some children at seven or eight and that the best thing to do to improve efficiency is to have the children practice. It is probably true that reading progress occurs as children get the opportunity to read. Thus, formalized periods of direct instruction may even be wasteful to the process of learning. Happily he also said that teaching reading could be the least instead of the most expensive part of the school program. It does not require the fancy materials that schools are currently buying. Doubling libraries and chances to read will pay off better except for a few who need closer help. Our objectives in reading should be: Does the child read independently? Does he use research materials? Does he select a book to keep at his desk?

(not) learning to read

pictureless picture books

64 Parents often ask how long they should allow their child to go on in school without a certain proficiency in reading. Research evidence seems to indicate that maturity rates and home background play an important part in a child's learning to read. I have frequently counseled that if a child does not learn to read in the first grade, it isn't a very serious problem. All kinds of factors may combine to prevent the so-called usual success in learning to read in grade one. Almost everything else in school eventually depends upon whether or not the child has learned to read. More important than this even is the fact that a child who doesn't learn to read well feels inadequate and a failure. My recommendation is that reading problems must be pinpointed and corrected by the fourth grade or else the child is in danger of falling behind at an ever-accelerating rate. Every decent school system must make adequate provision for remediation by the fourth grade or face the charge of educational incompetence. Every parent has the right to ask exactly what is being done to insure that his child will not leave fourth grade a reading failure.

Reading is not called the process of decoding the symbols of our language. Thus, our alphabet rearrangements, which eventually become meaningful words, are a code. The task of learning to read may, quite properly, be labeled decoding. Traditionally, children's books of the textbook or basal reader type and of the kind known as children's literature have been essentially picture books with text below. One of the problems children face as they start to learn to read or decode is that many words look like many other words, and frequently the child takes educated guesses. Just as in any code, guessing may have some value, but it can also lead to mistakes. When pictures accompany text, children often look at the pictures and try to guess what the words below may say about the picture above. Especially when children are having problems in reading, this tendency to guess at words based upon the pictures encourages inexactness. So, while I love picture books of high quality, there is some wisdom in recopying books on cards without the pictures above and forcing children to be precise.

censoring books

I should like to talk about censorship of books and movies in schools. There have always been attempts to burn the books or ban the movies. None have succeeded too well. I should not like to be misunderstood in the slightest. There are certain materials and films that I do not believe belong in the public realm. These are those materials that are clearly designed to appeal to base sexuality or perversion simply for the sake of sex or perversion. Oakies in Steinbeck's novels need to talk the way they do because their everyday language was vulgar and coarse by middle-class standards, but that is the way they talk, and to take those offensive words out of the book would be to perpetrate a lie larger than the attempt to censor. When a school shows a film that offends some portion of its clientele, the question to ask is not who or how many are offended, but whether there was truth and beauty in the film in spite of the offenses. I am not for open floodgates, but for waters of information and esthetics that are un-muddied by deliberate filth and hucksterism.

summer reading

Although 50 percent of the American people live within five miles of a library, only 5 percent use the library. Whether or not a child learns that the printed word is important depends largely upon his experiences with words in his family environment. Where reading is an important function of the family's life-style, success in reading is virtually guaranteed. If a library is within five miles of your home, an excellent family outing that will break the awful monotony of hour after hour of TV is a family trip to the library. Children can find the children's room; parents should tag along and encourage. Borrow from your library and bring the books home. In a week plan to return, and if you'll make this a habit, your children will have an experience. Ten minutes a day with preschool children will pay great dividends at the beginning of their school days. Try it and see for yourself.

helping your child to read

eyes and reading problems

66 If you have a child with a reading problem, and it is summer vacation time, and you are wondering what you can do to help at home, you should find these suggestions of value. If you can't get competent summer help, then I'd suggest you make a visit to a good bookstore and let your child pick out a half dozen of the wonderful paperbacks for children that are now available. Try this outing to the bookstore casually and not as your way to be sure he reads better. Remember, most people, including children, don't like to be done good to. Don't reject any choices he makes, and don't lament the cost—you can't make a better investment. Once home, try to set some specific time aside for him to read to you. Don't correct anything he reads, even if he makes an obvious error. If he asks, help. If not, be still. Don't look over his shoulder. Show much approval for any behavior that even approaches reading. In two months try to get him into as many books as he will choose. Reward him only after he's tried. Remember, if he has reading problems, he likely hates books. Don't force; let him choose his books, if he will.

Not infrequently a child's reading problems stem from eye difficulties. I rather vividly recall my youngster in her first year of junior high coming home with grades that reflected more than the expected age group's frequent inattention in school. Some probing produced a story that still amazes me because I had not thought to investigate the matter earlier. She said she couldn't see the chalkboard, and I immediately asked where she was sitting. It turned out that she was no more than twenty or so feet from the board, and I realized that, in fact, she could not see much at that distance. But before you go to an eye doctor, ask him these questions: (1) Do you make near-point vision tests on children? (2) Do you make visually related perception tests? (3) Do you provide vision training care for children with learning difficulties? (4) Will I get a report from you? If he answers all of these or three out of four affirmatively, then he can help your child with reading problems. If not, perhaps he can recommend someone who can.

inane "literature"

children read what they photograph

Many parents are awakening to the fact that their children may be getting an excellent education in many subjects but that language skills are sliding downhill. The reason is not simple. I would judge that few children are hearing or reading literature with beauty and complexity. While we plan elaborate and effective work for children in the sciences and social studies, a planned literature program in the elementary schools is unheard of. Thousands of children are slaving away at programmed materials that are not adequate at all for the task we are discussing. Their advantages are important for short, selected periods of time, but hour upon hour of reading only the most simple and inane English construction can do little to foster any sort of feeling for this magnificent English language. I would guess that some of this abject genuflecting before programmed materials comes from people who themselves have read little and care less for the literary experience. Until those who lead see, it will only be the blind leading the blind, and another generation of children will wither on the academic vine.

Some of you may recall that I have written about how children will want to read if they feel that what they are reading is what they think, feel, and say. Most of what children read in the traditional, basic textbooks is, of course, what others have written. On the surface and in general, this is perfectly acceptable. However, when children begin to read, it is particularly important that their interest be captivated and that they feel a certain urgency about the learning process. Can you imagine how a child must feel as he sees what he has said written on a chart? Well, in certain parts of New York children are armed with simple cameras and are taking pictures of everything and anything that captivates their interest. In effect the children are really taking the pictures for their own textbooks. To Morton Feinman of the New York City schools, congratulations for realizing that a picture is not only worth a thousand words, but in the hands of expert teachers and eager learners, it can become a thousand words. After all, the best learning and wisdom comes out of the mouths of babes.

what they need to know

the "new" social studies

68 A recent survey of 5,000 Connecticut school children indicates that youngsters crave the facts about alcohol, tobacco, drugs, and sex by the time they reach the fourth grade. Even nine- and ten-year-olds see drinking as a social problem, and they worry about lung cancer. Many sixth graders want to know enough so that they can make decisions in these areas. Though most twelve-year-olds do not approve of drugs and smoking, they do start to become aware of the credibility gap between what their parents say and do. In grades ten and twelve it was frightening to learn that there was a sophisticated acceptance and a partial approval of the drug scene. I think all of this adds up to the importance of local school boards making very certain not only that they have prescribed courses on drugs, alcohol, and tobacco, but that they see to it that the methods, materials, etc., are up-to-date, factual, and being used. You can get this report, called "Teach Us What We Want to Know," from the Connecticut State Department of Education, Hartford, Connecticut.

Do you remember the good old days when your children were studying the dates of the American Revolution or recounting the travels of explorers to the American shores? Well, in many places this "names and dates" approach to social studies is over. Social studies have undergone a revolution. The old idea is called the "didactic approach"; the new is the "questioning and skeptical approach." Once children learned the major events and causes of World Wars I and II; now the analytical method has swept some schools by storm. The method is sometimes called the "inquiry approach," because it seeks for the problems and dilemmas of society and even asks students to step into the shoes of Washington or Emperor Hirohito. For example, in Scarsdale, New York, students really analyze the statement that anyone can become president of the U.S. After eliminating the ineligibles, such as women, everyone under thirty-five, people without college degrees, non-Christians, people from "wrong" states, and other types of people with no chance at all, it was decided that in any one election year only 100 men were really available. The new social studies may even come your way.

the idiocy of tests

testing them to death

Shall we play games? Complete this statement: "A fair day is one that is . . ." what? The correct answer is "clear." Would it seem strange to you if some children answered, "When a teacher was fair to you," or if some child said, "When you go on rides; that kind of fair"? That is an example of a test of reading skills from one of the best known skills tests used in the schools — the Metropolitan Achievement Test. This type of question seems to be testing one's general level of word knowledge. Want to try another from the same test? Here we go! "To keep means to..." what? "Hold" is included in the answers and is considered the correct answer. Another word in the choices is "carry." Many children choose "carry" and justify the answer, saying that "if you want to keep it you better 'carry' it." Reading achievement tests can make or break a teacher or a school system. Many people depend upon them for appraisals of their school's teaching effectiveness. In my view, this is not too much of a yardstick. What do you think?

Are children material that is waiting to be molded? A lecturer at the Nottingham (England) College of Education feels that the standardized test so widely used in the United States is one of the main devices used to force students into a mold. She commented that Americans are obsessed with the need to evaluate and to test. We impose behavioral objectives upon helpless children rather than allowing them to be people. I am personally convinced that we have gone bananas about knowing where children are in some grim and vain search to discover whether or not our teachers are cheating the taxpayer. Believe me, one day in a roomful of second graders, even for a poor teacher, is enough of a tax on the human nervous system to deserve a pretty fat paycheck. We do not believe children should really develop at their own rate and according to their own interests. In England the open school approach is working well because no one is holding a time limit over their heads and insisting that at the end of one year everything should be perfect. Open education takes time and skill and confidence in the capacity of children. Besides, most American children aren't ready for too much freedom too soon.

school schemes for perfection

rewards for learning

70 You have probably wondered that if giving children rewards for studying arithmetic and reading is a successful teaching method, why isn't it adopted in all schools so that we might produce super students. Here's why. First, whenever anyone says he has the magic cure for disinterest in school or violin playing, you can bet it won't work for everyone for very long. Second, most schemes to insure perfect responses from children to the school environment usually mean throwing out of the classroom everything and anything that will interfere with the stated goal. Translated into very plain English, it means that programmed reading and arithmetic, programmed spelling, and whatever else can be converted into instant feedback systems will replace singing, art, music, talk, crafts — everything that smacks of the creative. Whatever really delights the soul is ruled out because delight interferes with the progress in the three Rs. Children are not automatons. They need more than hour upon hour of silent dedication to a text. Good education isn't regimentation and slavery.

Teachers do not seem to do any better when rewarded with monetary gains for their excellence in teaching. Children, however, seem to thrive under a regime that rewards them with tokens that are redeemable for cash or for the opportunity to do something that they like. In New York City the reading, writing, and arithmetic scores of children in two slum schools have been raised considerably by the use of what is known as a token economy. Children are given work at a level appropriate to their ability, and they advance as rapidly as they can, all the while being rewarded with tokens that are turned in for playing with a gerbil, learning a card game, or buying time to play bingo or watch *Sesame Street*. There are three novel features in this program: one, the liberal use of parents who work as a team with teachers; next, the continual involvement of the parents in the entire school process; and finally, the support of the entire administration. Sounds quite rosy, doesn't it?

art in schools

movement education

Have you ever stopped to realize that children work as long as adults do on any given morning without the traditional refreshment break? Well, if they can't have a break, they need some diversion from the normal, repetitive mental work they do for three and a half hours. Art is one of these vital activities that too many schools are abandoning in the name of financial problems. The sciences are only the means to living, while the arts are, in truth, the ends of living. It is easy to assess or be accountable for progress in math or biology, but to attempt to discern whether art experiences are paying off isn't quite so simple. One critic calls the attempt to assess the performance of children in school the "bang-for-the-buck" method of determining human performance. Art experiences give vent to feelings. No good school program scraps art and keeps arithmetic. No real educator believes that saving money at the expense of the feeling components of the curriculum is worth it. Be sure that art is part of your child's school life. Education in the arts increases human satisfaction like no multiplication can.

It seems that years ago the Greeks saw some real connection between the mind and the body. As man grew older (I did want to say progressed, but I wasn't sure it was an apt word, considering the world is the way it is), he became less and less interested in his body and more and more concerned with things—planes, mowers, rifles, and automobiles. The development of the body has generally been left up to the physical education people—the muscles boys, as it were—and as a result we have lost a great deal of interest in body development. This is not so, however, with the people of Joplin, Missouri, where a great deal of interest is now centered upon the relationship between learning and physical coordination. Movement education is not dead in other places either. In Oklahoma City young children are learning more about their body space—how to move, jump, and interact with their own body area. Many children have not learned how big or small their bodies are. Many who are not aware of their personal space bump into things, collide with people, and are often seen as clumsy. It is good to see a healthy concern for our bodies being developed in the young.

are eight years of school enough?

joyless school architecture

The Amish folk of Pennsylvania have the strange idea that eight years of school are enough for anyone. In fact, Amish schools employ as teachers those people who have only graduated from the eighth grade. In an effort to evaluate the achievements of these students taught by the eighth-grade graduates, Wayne Miller of the University of Michigan compared the performance of five different groups of children on the Iowa Test of Basic Skills. He compared Amish youngsters attending all-Amish parochial schools with Amish children attending public schools with a 100 percent Amish enrollment, Amish children in schools with less than 50 percent Amish enrollment, and non-Amish children in public schools with 50 percent or less Amish enrollment, and finally children in modern schools with no Amish students. Amish parochial school children made the highest mean scores of any in the five groups in both spelling and word usage. They placed second in arithmetic and second in reading comprehension. Something seems to be working. Is it culture, communication, or what?

The architects tell us that windowless schools have all kinds of advantages over those that have windows: for instance, consistent, comfortable temperatures may be maintained throughout the year; minimal distractions from outside noise are made possible, and thus children in urban areas don't have to hear the jets and trucks outside; there is, of course, more wall space to show children's work; and finally, in the event of an accident, there is no danger from flying glass. All of this is true. An antiseptic environment can be produced, but at what expense? As I look out of my study window now at about seven A.M. after torrential rains the night before, I see fluffs of cloud and streaks of blue, and my heart soars for the beauty of what may be the rest of the day. Antisepsis was the basis of having women give birth in sterile hospital rooms without their husbands. But, in the name of joy, that is changing in many places. Children need the light, the air, the sky, and the streets to add zest to life—even if some learning gets short shrift.

only one
nervous
system

choose
your
school

Do teachers need free periods? Too many of us think that all the teacher has to do is stand in front of children and blithely talk away. Teachers' salary negotiations throughout the country in the next few years will undoubtedly stress salary. In turn, school boards, I notice, are replying with demands for changed working conditions. For instance, in Utah one large school district is insisting on teachers working the traditional eight-hour day. I haven't heard anyone talking about credit for work done at home, however. Let's face it. Teaching isn't like any other job. Few are called upon to handle the myriad of emotional and learning problems of so many at one time. One of my favorite expressions says, "Teachers have only one nervous system to give for the community. When that is gone, you can't get a transplant." The free period is urgent for the mental health of both child and teacher. The tension of teaching requires free time and working days that are more nearly professional than technical.

I think Victoria, Canada, is on the threshold of an exciting innovation in its schools. Most of us as adults have a great deal of choice when it comes to the stores we shop in, the doctors and dentists we use, and the many other ways we pick and choose freely. But school children and their parents have no choice whatsoever about school philosophy and curriculum. Victoria has decided to give parents the choice of the public school they wish to send their children to. One school will be a strict, traditional type of school, with rigid discipline and all that goes with what we once called the good old school days. A paired school will be quite the opposite. It will be avant-garde, gung-ho progressive, with much choice for children. One phase of the idea that particularly appeals to me is the idea of choice even about special instruction for children. For example, if one school has a great music program, a parent may elect to send his child there. Whether or not the school you choose to use is in your neighborhood will be of little importance. You pay your taxes and take your choice.

middle schools   the good school

Whenever administrators of schools feel the ire of the public, they retreat to an odd position. Rather than really try to defend their usually reasonable practices, which they have arrived at after mature and professional consideration, they abandon what they have and institute something supposedly new that is designed to get the hound dogs off the scent. And thus the *middle school* came into being when people attacked the junior high concept. No one has been very happy about the fifth through eighth graders. These ten- through thirteen-year-olds have always been an educational prickle in the bed of roses of most school systems. What do we do when something doesn't seem to work? Instead of ameliorating the defects, educators tend to search about for a new gimmick that will be the magical cure-all. Most of the research I know—such as that of Soares and others in Connecticut and Alexander in Florida—tells me that middle-schoolers are merely junior high students with another name and that the feelings of worth of these children are significantly lower than those in regular schools. All that's new isn't necessarily best.

The traditional American high school has taught the children well. So well, in fact, that much of what is taught there is better than the kids can get in college, and the American university knows it. But that excellence in academics may not be as vital today as it was in 1959. After all, Sputnik scared the daylights out of us, so we spanked the schools to produce satellites and rockets to land men on the moon. And now that we have been there, what is there left to do? We still are a long way from making the school human. We still have too many schools where kids are numbers and teachers are textbooks wired for sound. Mini-schools are developing here and there as alternatives to the corporate structures schools have become. Their motto is, ''Think small and imitate.'' Schools ought not to be only dispensers of information and minor bureaucracies. Students need more than information. They need atmospheres where they live good lives, not frenetic races toward mathematical superiority.

social class and school success

patterns of destruction

By the time a British youngster is seven years old, social class and the environment that accompanies it have separated the winners from the losers in the school world. Ninety-two percent of 17,000 British school children were studied, and these are the amazing results. Working-class children are handicapped from birth. By the age of seven they are way behind middle-class children in mental development, reading, and schoolwork. Also, working-class youngsters are an inch shorter than middle-class contemporaries and more likely to have speech defects, too. It was found that the average gap in reading achievements between the children from homes where the fathers were unskilled workers and those whose fathers were in the professions was considerably more than two years. Later on the gap was so wide that a four-year difference between the children of the most unskilled fathers and the most highly educated ones was evident. Just as significant are the differences between the two groups regarding their attitudes toward teachers. The children of the working class showed definite hostility toward teachers, withdrawal and depression, and a marked writing-off of adult standards.

On Monday morning the school looked like a minor atomic bomb had hit. Nearly every room was a shambles. Ink flowed through the hall; typewriters were smashed; soap littered the floors; cardboard bulletins were torn to bits. A school had just been vandalized, and the authorities and the community were stunned and outraged. There is violence in the school by night and mad mayhem while school is in session. Violence in the schools is usually the work of people who are students of the school. It is their act of revenge for either real or imagined atrocities performed by the school staff. Vandalism patterns usually show that certain rooms are left untouched. Whose are they? Frequently they are the rooms of teachers who are known to not hassle the kids. What to do? First, a thorough survey of teachers' attitudes toward kids is urgent. All teachers who say they really hate the kids or who are super arrogant ought to be invited to transfer.

school vandals

i.q. test fallacy

76 Vandalism in the schools is a growing phenomenon. Kids don't willfully destroy places they like. They tend to tear up three rooms in succession and somewhat mysteriously leave certain adjacent rooms untouched. I have suggested thorough interviews with all teachers to determine their attitudes. Today, in this nation, we have plenty of teachers who would love the chance to teach the unteachables. All teachers who hate their assignment, particularly in junior high schools, ought to be urged to transfer to more sedate places with no hard feelings. Second, student councils that really operate and are meaningful need to have a share in governing. Sounds wild, doesn't it? But if the truth be known, kids are harder on themselves than are adults. A student-teacher curriculum study needs to immediately get under way to ascertain where the school is or isn't meeting real needs. Third, the community needs to start to enter the school as a potent force for good. Again, vandals aren't mafia types who have no way to amuse themselves on Saturday night. They are hostile, angry kids who know whom they hate.

I suppose I shall never forget a speech I gave in Salt Lake City in 1955 when I rather heatedly declared that there was a social class bias in better than 90 percent of the known I.Q. tests. I still have the letter from a prominent psychologist in the area who said that he had never heard a more disgusting presentation. Well, it isn't pleasant to hear refutation of one's own beloved ideas, not for him nor for anyone else. That was twenty years ago, my friends, and your children and mine are still taking the same old tests with the same old nonsense in them. For example, we have lately coined the idiotic terms of *over-achiever* and *under-achiever,* which mean, if you can believe it, that when a person's output is below what his test score says he can do, he is an under-achiever. Similarly, if teachers observe a child doing more than tests predicted he could, he is termed an over-achiever. Labels are libelous and too often only serve to make harsh judgments.

the joy of accomplishment

two kinds of happiness

A few years ago Charles Silberman's book *Crisis in the Schools* introduced the notion that schools were joyless places. As might be expected, school people all over took up the cry and started to demand from their curriculum planners school programs that were joyful. Little of learning can be just fun. There is joy in achievement, in sustained intellectual attention to an absorbing topic. But just plain fun in learning can too often be a diversion from learning activities that must be quite rigorous even for little kids. An old Latter-day Saint expression says, "man is that he might have joy." This means that man is not on earth to be morose and downhearted. Life is meant to be exhilarating and good. Little bags of learning tricks may make some learning fun, but the greatest joy that could come into the schools is evidence that children, each and every one of them, are mastering learning that is meaningful in their lives. True joy comes from a sense of accomplishment, of achieving what is often barely possible at first glance.

A dog and a rabbit are running in a field. On the surface they are doing the same thing. Both are running and each appears to be using his full capacity. In fact, there is a great difference between them with regard to the motivation for their activity. One is happy, the other unhappy. The dog is happy because he is chasing the rabbit and there is some hope of achieving. The rabbit is unhappy because he is being pursued, and he is afraid. When the rabbit has reached a burrow and the dog can't get him, he is safe and thus happy, and the dog is unhappy because he has not achieved. There are two kinds of happiness. One is based on escape from danger; the other is based on fulfillment of hope. The second, fulfillment of desire, is the only true happiness. The happiness achieved through fear is too often the happiness children find in school. They learn but only after much fear and restraint. They need to learn joyously so that what they learn motivates them and helps them want to learn more.

untapped wisdom

living with a creative child

78 In the March 1971 *PTA Magazine* is a most unusual story that rather neatly illustrates the point that there is much untapped wisdom in children. Steve Neuman, ten years old, of West Bend, Wisconsin, became deeply interested in the book on the human heart that he was reading for his science class. To practice what he had learned, he applied his ear to his little brother's chest and listened. "That sounds odd," he thought. He told his mother he thought, from what he had read, that little Jackie had a heart disorder. Mother took Jackie to the doctor, and sure enough, Steve was right. At last report the doctors were preparing Jackie for open-heart surgery. And that's what little brothers are for. It has been well said that the child is father to the man. It has also been said that out of the mouths of babes comes wisdom. In today's scientific world, where children are learning what ages of old never guessed at, you can never tell when great discoveries will be made.

While the whole world cries for creativity in its people, parents might well be warned that rearing a creative child isn't the easiest thing in the world. In the first place, the truly creative child (and in this context I do not mean creative in a particular field of human endeavor but rather one who is super-intelligent) continually tries to outsmart adults. The process of withstanding this intellectual onslaught can be hard on the ego of any adult. It is not that the child means to be mean; it is only that he finds it necessary to contest whatever information or ideas anyone produces. The total approach of this type of child is distinctly different and unorthodox. These children have to experience everything firsthand. They will not accept secondhand versions of any human experience. As a result, they get into plenty of trouble because they make lots of trials and errors. In school creative children bypass conventional answers and frequently come up with their own solutions to problems that teachers and peers don't see. How to live with this child? He must be accepted for what he is, and he needs patience and guidance because of his immaturity.

classes for the gifted

We have discussed children with unusual gifts, children who at a very young age seem to have an unusual command of their destiny. In general I don't approve of special classes for gifted children because most of them do not turn out to be very special during the regular course of their lives. They will usually be forced to live in the world with the rest of us. While they remain in regular school classes, they need opportunities to go beyond what the school ordinarily provides. They need opportunity to dabble in foreign language, in mathematics, science, and other academic realms in such a way that it falls within the ordinary school day. Whatever is meaningful for the average child is doubly meaningful for the gifted one. Some experts advocate skipping this type of youngster so that he may graduate from high school by age fifteen. While everything about the child is accelerated, I would not skip him too often unless it is also perfectly clear that his emotional development reasonably matches his mental growth. Intellectual precocity does not often breed social advantage.

nonverbal messages

We communicate with children in a variety of nonverbal ways; that is, we send messages to children about how we feel about them by how we look at them, how we touch them, how we stand before or near them. For instance, when we beam approvingly at the child who does what we want him to do, we tell him, though not in so many words, how we really feel about him. Similarly, when we sort of ''look through'' certain children who don't appeal to us or when we look over or away from children we really dislike, we don't fool them at all. If you want to try a bit of an experiment, try looking as if you were looking at those whom you adore at some children with whom you have contact but whom you really don't care for very much. When we touch children with the ends of our fingers, our hands rigid and palms flexed upward, we communicate our feelings as surely as if we had said, ''Oh, you are a snivelling little beast!'' No matter what our mouths say, our unspoken gestures, touches, and eye contact tell children precisely how we really feel about them.

your body talks   what words cover up

80 There is much behavior in classrooms that can be considered nonverbal. Nothing is said, yet a message is sent that is unmistakable to both teacher and learner. Let's take a look at a few of these, beginning with eye contact: If a student avoids it, he is sending a silent message that says, "Don't call on me." Eye contact with the teacher sends the message that the student is open to communication with you. Arm extensions communicate feelings on the part of the lecturing teacher. A study found that, other things being equal, students in classes where professors used extended arms often learned more than those in classes where this was not the case. Nodding teachers, and I don't mean those who are sleeping, encourage their students more than teachers who don't nod. But if they nod too regularly, all of the good gets cancelled. By around the fourth grade students learn that how they raise their hands to volunteer tells the teacher how much they want to say. Finally, where a teacher stands tells his class whether he wants them to respond and how much. Teachers who stay behind their desks tell their students nonverbally that a close relationship is not desired. What body language do you use at home, at work?

There are those children who talk a blue streak both at home and at school. Not surprisingly this unusual verbosity can be a ruse of the child to cover up inadequacies in other areas of learning. Frequently when a child finds little or no success in manipulative activities, he will retreat behind a barrage of words. Verbal expertise is a valued skill, and the only time it ought to be thought of as a negative trait is if it is accompanied by clear deficiencies in other areas. Children who have retreated into a waterfall of words do so because they lack the motivation to try other activities since trying may induce a failure experience. These children need slow but steady adult assurances that to try will not necessarily mean failure. This means that what they try must almost be pretested to assure nonfailure. These children often fool us and themselves because they possess a skill, verbal ability, a trait highly prized by the adult world. Thus, adults are dazzled by the child's verbal pyrotechnics, and his real deficiencies are camouflaged.

modifying behavior

the shy child

In the last few years a number of terms have been bandied about the psychological world that need to be more clearly defined for the public. Many parents are seeing and hearing that their children are being tossed candies for the good behavior they exhibit in the classroom. These rewards are meant to induce the children to perform again in the same manner. It is hoped that children will eventually alter any past behavior that has been causing difficulty. The technique of offering rewards for work done well is called reinforcement, and it is the result of behavioral psychology. Previously children who exhibited unwanted behavior were reprimanded, cast out, or psychoanalyzed. None of these methods worked well. Behavioral management techniques have utilized tangible rewards that have changed behavior in some remarkable ways. They have been most effective. All parents need to be alert to the importance of the tangible rewards' being slowly reduced and replaced by social rewards, such as approval of peers or of teachers.

Our society seems to value, even worship, children who are outgoing, lively, and loquacious. The shy child is nearly considered a dreaded child. And yet, shyness, which is related to temperament, is for many children their life-style. They can no more become outgoing and vivacious than tadpoles can become frogs overnight. In fact, that is a very bad analogy, come to think of it, because tadpoles inevitably become frogs, while shy children don't inevitably become loud and lively. Shyness is only a problem when the adult world starts to label it and bug the child about his reticence. There is no real reason to feel unhappy about being shy unless the adults around force you to the wall. Parents who push a child to become the vigorous type don't help but, in fact, embed this quality deeper into the child. On the other hand, some parents learn to run interference for the shy child; thus he never learns to respond to life on his own terms. You cannot judge a child's future happiness by whether or not he is a superstar at the conversation table.

diagnosing learning problems

when they can't learn

82 At a meeting of the Association for Children with Learning Disabilities, it was reported that as many as 80 percent of delinquent boys may have begun their troubled lives because of a potentially correctable learning problem. Jane Brody in the *New York Times* reported that most teachers and psychologists allow these kinds of children to go through school undiagnosed. The problem affects five boys to every one girl and should be readily identifiable when the seemingly bright child remains years behind his age mates in nearly all subject matter in the elementary school. Emotional problems in these children are the result of learning difficulties and not the cause of them. These children see and hear well, but something in what may be termed the circuitry of their brains doesn't allow information that is fed to the brain to be processed properly. Usually these children need individual attention and teaching methods that require the use of all of the senses.

When a child has problems in school, it is not a stigma but a learning problem. Most of the children with generalized learning problems—that is, they seem to not be able to handle the variety of concepts school children usually catch onto pretty well—are not mentally retarded, but they have difficulties with perception, concepts, or coordination. Two things can be of great help to these children. One is plenty of household chores that involve the practice of hand-eye coordination, and the second is plenty of practice of these chores. Where a child needs some feelings of importance but doesn't get them from his school failures, home tasks can be made fun and prove to be success building. If hand-eye coordination is needed, pouring, slicing, beating, snapping beans, peeling, hulling, and folding napkins really help. Setting the table develops left-right coordination as does sorting gloves or sorting shoes for shining. A child who can't catch a small ball can catch a large pillow or sweater rather easily. Those in the home can do more than they think to build the skills necessary to a child before learning can take hold. Try it.

learning disabilities

who's retarded?

Many an intelligent child develops learning disabilities that become quite apparent in the elementary and early junior high school years. Then, and often suddenly, the two-year gap between his age and his school performance narrows until there isn't a gap anymore. But it isn't always that way; in fact, it is more often that he fails more and more because of the continual accusations that he is "lazy" and "not settling down to work," and that he could do it if "only he would try." After about two or three years of school, these comparisons, urgings, and defamatory remarks start to catch hold of the developing personality, and he becomes as difficult to like as he is to teach. His learning disability must be caught, taught, and explained to him so he can understand that he is neither peculiar nor stupid. It is remarkable how much he can be hurt by the barrage of negative responses he receives from all those with whom he works, plays, and lives. If he has been damaged enough by these remarks and hasn't learned to read by the age of thirteen, then it is nearly too late to do much to help him.

Disproportionate numbers of minority group children are labeled mentally retarded and assigned to special classes even though they do not belong there. This is no plot to relegate minority kids to academic limbo. This misplacement is the result of a poor assessment system based upon I.Q. tests that are unfair to other than the middle-class child. When 268 children in special classes were reevaluated, 75 percent of the youngsters would not have been categorized as mentally retarded. If the following changes are made in evaluation procedures, there will not be so great a disproportion of minority children classified as retarded: (1) an I.Q. score of seventy instead of seventy-five to eighty-five should be used as a point of division between assignment to regular classes and those for the retarded; (2) the adequacy of a child's performance outside of school should be taken into account; and (3) sociocultural factors should be taken into account when interpreting scores. All labeling isn't bad, but more accurate labels are urgently needed; forgetting anyone's special needs will be a step backward. More fair assessments of a child's total behavior are essential.

teaching the retarded

neurologic learning disability syndrome

84 Thanks to a new breed of educators, parents with mentally retarded children need not hide their children in back rooms. Today all over America the mentally retarded are being trained through a philosophy that says that patience and expectation add up to performance. The learning of conceptual skills such as arithmetic and language cannot be successful before physical control and performance are achieved. When teachers believe firmly that children can learn and that they will learn, given time, materials, and dogged persistence, they do learn. When teachers do not have more than seven to a class, when materials and physical space are designed just for them and are not revamped regular classrooms, there will be learning. When teachers have carefully selected goals for each child and when they design the learning experiences to aim precisely at these goals, there is every likelihood that children will learn what is expected. Starting where the child is and taking him to where he isn't is an intelligent and humane way to educate.

Although it is fairly common knowledge that children grow and achieve at their own pace, and that eventually they grow out of most of their childhood problems, there are hundreds of thousands of school children who will not grow out of their inability to learn spelling, math, and reading. I don't know how many times I have heard teachers sigh and say, "He seems bright enough; he just doesn't try." For many children who are lagging behind in school, all of these explanations are quite precise. Nearly 3 percent of the children who are such problems will never catch up, never make up for their apparently childish inability to learn. These children are victims of what is now termed *neurologic learning disability syndrome*. They have normal intelligence, but some mysterious failure in the child's neurology prevents him from mastering the complexity of the three Rs. It is reliably estimated that this syndrome causes school failure, emotional disturbance, and juvenile delinquency.

hurrying learning   what retards learning

85

There are some natural stages of child development that cannot be bypassed by any of the pressure-cooker means that too many schools are foisting upon children. A few weeks ago in New York the famed Swiss psychologist, Jean Paiget, warned that too many schools are trying to hurry the pace of learning by skipping stages. Background and environment do play an important role in accelerating or retarding learning. No matter how fast the pace, however, all children need to pass through the same phases of understanding. One teacher reported that many parents in the school in which she teaches drill their kids on the alphabet but forget to teach them to tie their shoelaces. While the children are ready to learn shoelace tying, they often are not ready for reading. Let me quote Professor Paiget directly: "We need pupils who are active, who learn early to find out by themselves, partly by their own spontaneous activity and partly through materials we set up for them. The principal goal is to create men who are capable of doing new things." A good mixture of subtlety and structured learning activities will help accomplish this.

Deprivation of either emotional or physical needs is serious. A study at Yale University showed that when children were seriously deprived of warm adult relationships, they sought these in school. The effect of this lack of adult attention and affection is so strong that it prevents learning. It has been thought that a lack of brains or motivation is the most serious thing that retards learning. While it is true that either or both may interfere with learning, it is fairly clear that the deprived child will do almost anything to gain the attention he needs even if it means not learning. All of this goes back to the well-proven, if perhaps not the best-proven, theory that it is our personal, emotional needs that take precedence over almost everything we wish to achieve. If we see ourselves as inadequate humans, we cannot settle down long enough to learn anything. Learning, then, is related to our good feelings about ourselves. When anyone feels as if he is good for nothing, he surely will be.

leading the blind   hail, dyslexia

86 If you ever want to see an inspiring thing, then try to visit a school or behavior modification center where children who have never before been helped to speak, to look, or to react become changed through techniques that reward their good behavior and generally disregard their bad behavior. As strange as this may sound, I have seen astounding results. But most delightful of all is the scene I witnessed when I saw a mentally retarded fifth grader sitting near a mentally retarded first grader and helping the little guy learn to read. Here was one who wasn't very competent at all; indeed, he was by most usual standards incompetent, yet he was teaching another child the little he knew. And he took his job seriously, never diverting his attention, always being thoughtful and kind though firm. He was, in short, the very perfect model of what we train highly competent college youth to become. The blind apparently can lead the blind if one of them has but a little sight.

In certain areas of the country it has become fashionable to have one child with braces on his teeth and another with dyslexia. Dyslexia is the term used to describe children who have apparently normal intelligence but for some reason have not learned to read. There seems to be little professional agreement upon the meaning of the word, the symptoms, the number of children affected, and the cure for the condition. What has happened is that once a child is so labeled, too many people just sit back and seem content that they know what is wrong. To many educators this is a very unproductive attack on the problem of the intelligent child who has not learned to read. In fact, in many places the dyslexic child has the disease label attached to him, and then he vegetates in classrooms waiting for the disease to go away. Regardless of the label, these signs point to reading problems that should be attacked using every known reading methodology: reading performance at least two years below grade and intelligence level, even though eyes and intelligence are normal; problems in learning by sight method; poor performance in oral reading; and difficulty in distinguishing between *b* and *d* and *p* and *q*.

overcoming handicaps

your mental age

Some years ago a quadriplegic student entered my classes at the university to prepare to become a teacher. Our department was astounded. How could a person with all four limbs immobile hope to teach children? Twenty years ago doctors told Carol Loftis to leave Warm Springs, Georgia, and resign herself to a life of dependence such as one would expect from a carrot. Not for Carol. She plugged away aided by legions of "sloppy, sentimental" college students who thought she just might make it with a little bit of luck and some old-fashioned pluck. And she did. Two years ago this multiply handicapped girl graduated with honors as a fully certified teacher. No job loomed on the horizon until a few weeks ago when the Salt Lake City Board of Education used their heads and their hearts and entered into an agreement with the Primary Children's Medical Center to hire Carol to teach hospitalized children. Bravo to them and to Carol. America rejoices with you.

The term *mental age* is intimately tied to the concept of intelligence that was sharply defined by a man named Binet. Let's see if we can understand it. Children's powers increase as they get older. There is nothing new or startling about this. It is common knowledge. They become more capable, better organized, better in their judgment. In other words, you would hate to send a four-year-old on an errand that a six-year-old could manage competently. Well, when a four-year-old does the job a six-year-old manages competently, then he most certainly may be said to be performing like a six-year-old with respect to the particular task he undertook. His birthday age or chronological age is four; his competence to perform this errand is age six. It is further likely that in many other tasks he will perform as a six-year-old. Therefore, he has a mental age of six and a real or chronological age of four. Thus normality in intelligence means that for every year a child has been alive he makes one year progress in mental ability. If, however, he outruns his earthly years by three months, mentally he has an I.Q. of 125. Complicated? Yes and no.

who knows english

wellsprings of bigotry

88 When 86,000 youngsters and 8,000 young adults were given the opportunity to write essay-type answers, an analysis of this enormous number of papers showed that only four or five people out of this many had a good command of the English language. This is a startling and astounding report. The writing samples of nine-year-olds showed almost no mastery of basic writing mechanics. The thirteen-year-olds showed a nearly complete lack of understanding of written language. Seventeen-year-olds showed a sound grasp of the basics of written language, though spelling and word choice were weak. Young adults in the twenty-six to thirty-five range were not even willing to put pen to paper, many of them turning in one-line answers. Sixty percent of this age group made spelling errors. I conclude some things from this report. The older we get, the more relevant our language seems to us. Children probably write too little in school and read less outside of their usual texts. No attention to a planned children's literature program is attempted, so children never hear anything but the drivel of their programmed reading texts.

It is not difficult to create bigotry in children. When parents openly exclude people different from them from their company, children model themselves after this. Most frequently bigotry serves as a person's partial solution to his own feelings of inadequacy. Rarely do secure children hate others. All children search for emotional security and ego identity. When problems arise in life, the individual may seek a variety of ways of solving the problems. The fully functioning person analyzes the difficulty and proposes ways of meeting it with a degree of reality. Children are prone to lay the blame on someone or something rather than facing it squarely. Usually some out group becomes the butt of their scorn. A simple example involves what boys and girls in the fourth grade often do. Each sex blames the other for the noise. Transferring the source of the problem isn't at all unusual. A common expression says, "The poor workman blames his tools." A poor person often blames a poorer person for his poverty. It takes maturity to recognize reality.

the biology of sex differences

boys and girls are different

How is it that little girls tend to play with dolls and little boys throw footballs around? Is it simply a matter of each sex following the traditional patterns they have seen each sex perform? Well, to some degree this is true. There is no fear necessary in little boys doing female type things such as washing dishes, and there are likely to be no adverse effects from little girls playing football. The fact of the matter is that, culture aside, little boys and girls do play differently. Piaget, the great Swiss researcher, asks, "How much is instinct, and how much imitation of what the child appreciates in its own mother?" There is nothing inherently wrong with children identifying themselves with people of the same sex. It is not a male or female plot. It is, for lack of a better term, the natural order of things. Children can easily exchange roles, but there is a certain biological point from which there is no digression. Parents who attempt to raise their little girls to be boys and vice versa are doing these children a great disservice.

Any discussion about children and their identification with specific sex roles undoubtedly leaves some people wondering, others angry. Let me clarify, if I may. The endocrine systems of males and females are different. There are some readily observable differences between males and females, if not psychologically, at least physically. Anyone who tries to refute this basic fact is simply blind to what is patently obvious. It is important for girls to identify with their own sex models. The same is true for boys. Pushing children into unnatural sex roles is foolhardy and dangerous. The real issue that confronts us is more related to the absolute split that has existed between men and women and our concepts of what is proper for each to do at home and at work. There is no shame in a boy doing dishes, baking, cleaning, or playing with dolls. I am certain, however, that he shouldn't play that he is the mommy. He isn't; he can't ever be, and he shouldn't be. His proper role is father, and in this he needs to be loving and tender. There is a male-female difference, and long live the difference.

89

when little boys play at being girls

boys fail

90 If little girls want to be tomboys, we really don't make too much of a fuss over it because we know that someday they will outgrow it. But when a little boy says he wants to be a girl, or if he starts to play with little girls or even dress up like a girl, wow! There is trouble in the home in the adult world. How should an adult, mature parent behave when a boy expresses some of these desires and interests? Certainly not with horror or shock. It is true that much of our sex role—that is, how we know how to behave as a little boy or girl—is learned. In nearly all cases of growing up, children learn their proper sex role from mothers and fathers and their community. Sometimes little boys want to behave like girls because they want the tenderness accorded girls by society. A parent ought to help a child express his deep feelings for wanting to be better loved. Help him air his doubts and cope with his own feelings. Facing feelings at three may resolve some problems at twenty-three.

From Boston's Judge Baker Guidance Center comes the fascinating report that failure in school is almost exclusively a male affliction. In a study of learning disabilities of eight- to fifteen-year-olds of average and superior intelligence, boys were educationally retarded in an eight to one ratio. The boys in this study who were educationally retarded showed the following characteristics: they were neurotically anxious about growing up, assuming the male role, and maturing through learning. The following parental practices appear to create this fear of learning: the mother's fear of maleness; one or both parents' repression of the child's male drives because they see this as an expression of hostility; derogation of the child as a learner; conflicting parental attitudes toward learning; and finally, the presence of an antisocial or criminal family secret. The final conclusion of this group is that almost half of the school children who are unable to learn are suffering from fears of maturation, fears of growth, and fears of sexual identification and are thus stifled in reaching their intellectual potential.

educating male six-year-olds

male teachers

Lest I be accused of sexist tendencies, here is a report done by two females at the Laboratory School at Northern Illinois University that concludes that boys of six years of age are better off being educated in all-male classes than in coeducational situations. In all-boy classes, boys were investigative and manipulative. In coeducational classes, six-year-old boys were less willing to share themselves. In coed classes, boys were more of a behavior problem because girls dominated the classroom scene. In all-boy classes, boys were very physical, and learning accompanied their motor activity. In coed classes, boys had a particularly hard time with handwriting and desk work. And on the playground there was much conflict as girls tended to disagree with the boys' standards of playground behavior. In all-boy classes, boys were outspoken and insisted on input, but they shrank back in coed classes. Finally, in all-boy groups, boys settled disputes with dispatch, their messages being open, direct, and swift. All of this means that there are some alternatives to be considered in the education of young boys.

When there is a male teacher in an elementary school classroom, the girls are girlier, and the boys are more masculine. In America today the father figure is very much absent. American fathers are usually "up and at 'em" figures in most households. After all, it is still mother who stays home in the typical family, and father becomes a weekend and nightly visitor. I trust I have not unfairly characterized the American father. At any rate, our focus here is on the importance of the male teacher in the elementary school. Here he provides a constant presence, and (if he is a "male" male) the evidence is that while the children may not do better academically, a psychological gain is observed. In essence, children seem to feel better about themselves when male teachers are part of their experience in school. In wise schools efforts are made to recruit the brightest, most virile young men to teach elementary school. Though classrooms will be noisier and not so neat, I personally advocate the use of male teachers in even the lowest primary school classes.

male chauvinism in basal readers

children and divorce

92 A group known as the Women on Words and Images has done an exciting job of culling from 134 elementary school basal readers examples of female stereotypes that pervade the hallowed pages of basal reader land. Their conclusion: These books are overwhelmingly male oriented. Their major thesis is that male chauvinism starts in the kindergarten. Some of their results show that boys outnumber girls in stories by five to two. Boys outnumber girls four to one in stories showing ingenuity, perseverance, strength, creativity, bravery, apprenticeship, earning money, competitiveness, and exploration. Girls exhibit such traits as passivity, docility, and dependency six times as often as boys. Girls rarely venture far from the hearth, while boys lead adventurous lives. My only objection to the study is that I find it hard to consider these things sexist because I believe that there was never any intent to demean females. Males and females are different in many important ways, and they shall always be so.

In the welter of statistics about divorce and its effect on children, I feel that too many child development specialists have given the impression that divorce is better for the children than prolonged disturbance in the home. While this may on the surface be true, a recent study of 1,500 emotionally disturbed children, reported in the *Archives of General Psychiatry,* indicates that the aftermath of divorce is so devastating to youngsters that courts ought to appoint competent psychiatric help in most divorce cases involving children. While a certain strain and tension may indeed be removed by a couple's divorcing, there is an emotional cost that children pay no matter what the circumstances of the divorce may be. One group of researchers urges us to look at divorce as a prolonged trauma that can affect the character development of children. Divorce is not a process, not just an event. It is very frequently the cause of psychopathological disturbances in children.

childhood ulcers

extra-small children

When 300 children, aged three to fourteen, with peptic ulcers were studied recently, it was found that these were special kinds of children. They were what we might define as sensitive children who, at an early age, were placed under great and chronic stress. Once upon a time ulcers were a disease of the driving, up-and-coming, career-type man or woman, but in the last fifteen years it has become the favorite affliction for our school-dominated, excellence-oriented society. The combination most likely to produce ulcers in children at so tender an age is a strong drive to become tops at school coupled with an intense need for approval and affection. Some children who need both of these do not seem to develop ulcers. They just strive, push folks around, beat their way into the hearts of those who live with them, and survive quite well. But when the child is hypersensitive by nature, then the combination of the need to excel and the desire to be loved can spell ulcers.

There are some children who are exceptionally short for their age. Though they may not be classified as midgets, they are, by the time they are ten or so, very conscious of the fact that they are far smaller than their age mates all around them. There are a number of possible reactions of these children to their lives. Being small may (1) give them the notion that they can play baby for a far longer period of time than most others; (2) lead to resentment against their peers and parents or denial of the condition; or (3) lead them to isolate themselves out of a sense of shame. All of these mechanisms are not likely to help them in their adjustment to life. Whenever there is an abnormality in a child's development, the best course of action is to face the problem openly and squarely. Small children, like fat children, may easily develop reactions to the teasing of their peers, so parental wisdom and openness are vital.

93

childhood diabetes

accident prone?

94

Childhood diabetes is not the dreaded disease it was once. Both diet regulation control and insulin treatment allow the child to live a reasonably normal life. There is one aspect of the child's growth and development that should receive a great deal of attention from parents and school adminstrators. At a meeting of the Association of American Physicians, it was reported that childhood diabetics develop impairment of sensory perception within two years of the onset of the disease. The study of fifty-three diabetics, all of whom developed the disease in childhood, indicated that all senses were impaired in the diabetic as compared with children of the same age who were not diabetic. This means that the senses of touch, sight, and taste diminished early in the disease. I have never believed in being an alarmist. This does not mean that these senses seriously deteriorate or even moderately diminish in acuity. It simply means that as compared with a normal child they are impaired. Schools ought to know when children are diabetic and keep watchful eyes on their sense development.

For years we have used the term "accident prone" in relation to children who repeatedly had accidents. Now a professor of psychiatry at Columbia University says that heredity, not the unconscious wish to hurt oneself, may be a factor in accidents. Dr. William Langford's study of children who had many accidents over a twenty-year period showed that 70 percent of accident-repeating children came from families that had high accidental injury or death patterns. There seems to be no difference whatever between the brain activity, intelligence, or physical or emotional home environment of the two groups of children, except that the accident-high children were doers or action oriented. The study interestingly indicated that accident repeaters were fun to know, had an innate spirit of high adventure, and were competitive and impulsive. Generally the study showed that accident repeaters tended to be children who overreached themselves. Accident repeaters have a lot going for them, but it hurts.

lying

suicide among children

One of the games that children play is lying. They lie for a number of reasons. First, they lie because the penalty for wrongdoing is too severe. Next, they lie for attention. Some lie to get revenge, others to gain recognition. Overly harsh parents make telling the truth for children particularly painful. I have no objection to punishing children. When the family gets caught in severe punishment relationships, such as spanking, extreme deprivation of privileges, or hateful remarks from the parents regarding the child's moral stature, children learn to lie rather than face what may be, and certainly seems to them to be, grossly unfair punishment. If all else fails, tell a whopper and Mom will be sure to give you plenty of heed. Lying behavior often occurs to frustrate parents who get caught in the game of locking up the whole house so things won't get taken. Children who feel insignificant also lie so that they become important.

While it is a rarity to read of children under the age of ten threatening to commit suicide and even more of a rarity to have them make the attempt, it is a problem that needs to be met with patience, understanding and intelligence. The young child who threatens to kill himself is indicating a symptom of a seriously disturbed personality. Usually this kind of child is caught in a trap that to him seems impossible. One of the reasons that children will threaten to kill themselves is because below the age of ten the concept of death has a certain reversibility about it. That is, the young child sees death as reversible and not as a permanent thing. Thus, he can threaten, even attempt, death with the rather certain knowledge that he won't really die or that if he does, he will not be dead long. What causes children to threaten suicide? Parental pressures for excellence beyond the capacity of the child; concern of children over either delayed or precocious sexual development; the loss of a parent; or using suicide as weapon designed to manipulate parents.

emotionally disturbed children

coping with emotional problems

96

If ever there was a crisis in the field of mental health, it's now. There seems to be an urgency about putting our own house in order that is somewhat reminiscent of pre-World War II days when isolationism was a dirty word. In the last four years the number of emotionally disturbed children placed in state or county institutions has doubled. A startling fact is that 25 percent of these children will remain in custodial care for at least fifty years. At the present time there are 54,000 ten- to fourteen-year-olds living in mental hospitals in the United States. For the most part juvenile delinquents who return to court time after time are emotionally disturbed, and they are being relegated in institutions that, for the most part, are understaffed and underfinanced. Let us remember that when a child continually commits antisocial acts, he is screaming for help. What he gets is punishment from a society that cares far more for almost anything but sick people. Again I call for statewide appointment of commissioners of children who will have the authority to supersede other authorities where the welfare of children is concerned.

When every twentieth child admitted to a pediatric hospital was carefully examined, fifty-one out of eighty randomly selected children were found to have emotional difficulties warranting psychiatric consultation. This is one of the most startling findings I have run across in a long time. It tells me a number of things. First, it says that children admitted to pediatric facilities are there ostensibly for physical ailments, but it is possible that these physical symptoms are really part of severe emotional difficulties. More frighteningly, it tells me that it is entirely possible that more children are emotionally disturbed than we ever expected. On the other side of the argument, it may confirm the long-held idea that once a person is placed in a psychiatric setting, he is predicted to be more psychiatrically ill than he would be in a nonpsychiatric milieu simply because the doctors are finding what they expected to find or were looking for. It also suggests that pediatricians are not sufficiently trained in the identification of emotional disorders in children.

fear of hospitals   sick and in bed

Many parents, fearful of adding anxiety to their children's lives, delay until the very last second telling their children about medical treatment they are due to undergo. When children are going to the dentist for an extraction or to hospital for surgery, it is important to create a little stress. If children are given four to seven days to get used to the idea of what lies ahead, they will not spend all that time brooding but will use that time to rehearse their fears. Anticipation of pain is an important part of preparing for it. If it is hospitalization that is required, parents can expect the under-five child to be most frightened about separation from his parents. He may need time to talk much about this so that he can face it. The five- to nine-year-old is usually afraid of the needle and the actual surgical procedure, and the ten- to thirteen-year-old worries about his loss of control during the operation and his possible death. If children are deceived about pain, about the trauma of separation, then parents can expect more severe emotional responses. Stress is a part of human existence. It is part of the maturing process.

The bedridden or seemingly forever-sick child who spends at least a month or more away from the usual school routine is often a source of great dismay and disappointment to his parents. You needn't fret, however, because there is good evidence that isolation forced by illness often acts as a stimulant to the child's personal development. In America's aquanaut program where men spend much time together submerged below the surface of the ocean, it was found that the more time an aquanaut spent sick in bed as a child, the better he tended to perform as an aquanaut. The reasoning behind this strange tale is that the more time a child spends in bed, alone and away from his peer group, the more he models himself after the adults who surround him. The adult world usually presents a higher standard of achievement than the child would find in his peer group. Children who excel as adults have frequently developed work and success patterns that are adult. This "Teddy Roosevelt effect" seems to be valid and a source of comfort to those whose children are often ill.

when a child is dying

and thus they perish

98 Perhaps the saddest event in any human being's life is the death of a child. The child below the age of three has no concept of his personal death, so parents need not be concerned for the child's own anguish. What he does respond to in a very real way is the grief and torment that his parents and family may exhibit. The toddler cannot bear the burden of his parents' grief, so for children below the age of three, it is imperative that parents try not to communicate their own personal sense of devastation. As the child approaches five and six, he is becoming more aware of himself as an entity, and thus death does present a fearsome reality. Unfortunately hospitalization and approaching death often turn the child toward reflecting upon the many things he did that were wrong and for which he now thinks he is being punished. He needs to be reassured often that he is not rejected, that he is not being punished for the wrongdoings of the past. The awesome question of ''Will I die?'' should be answered directly with ''We all will, but you will not die today or tomorrow.'' Thus he can deny death yet know that it is coming. To the end he needs the support of everyone in his life.

Adults have difficulty in facing children with knowledge of the child's imminent death. As harsh and cruel as it may seem, I still remember the haunting words of a little boy who, suffering from leukemia and fretted over by two worried young parents, was taken out for what his parents knew to be his last ride to get a hamburger at a nearby stand. Too weak to take a bite, he turned to his parents, who could barely control their anguish and who were in danger of losing their own religious precepts, and said, ''Mommy, I'll finish my hamburger in heaven.'' Too shocked to reply, these two had learned the simple lesson of faith from out of the mouth of a babe, their son for whom they had been, perhaps, too solicitous. Parents who accept counsel in these matters learn that children, like adults, at first deny the fact of their imminent death, then are angry, bargain for more time, get depressed, and finally accept their fate quite cheerfully. Bless the children.

new leukemia treatment

living with leukemia

It is thrilling to hear that ten years ago the average life expectancy of a child stricken with leukemia was six months to a year, and that now with improved chemotherapy he can live five years more. One accompanying problem, however, is that now that more patients are living, more hospitals are finding that they have fewer beds available. Memorial Hospital in New York has done something about this, and it makes some real sense. Instead of keeping children with leukemia in the hospital, which is usually a rather dismal experience, the parents are taught fully about their child's condition. The child becomes an outpatient. He does not need to be hospitalized, but he does need constant surveillance and attention. Relapses in leukemic children are not unusual, and so the subject is now part of the education given a child's parents; they are taught how to observe signs of relapse and when hospitalization is indicated. Children with this type of cancer are now living their lives in the real world of other children instead of being cloistered in hospitals where they begin to feel they are incarcerated.

In a very real sense we are all facing death, someday. But children with leukemia face it with a more insistent reality than those of us who know that, barring accidents, we'll live to be about seventy or more. There are two schools of thought about children who are dying from leukemia. One school would not even say it that way; instead, they would say that some children are living with leukemia. The stress in a family caused by the knowledge of a dread disease is immense and can be overwhelming if the family makes frantic efforts to teach its members to face this death calmly. Both schools agree that those who are hardest hit are not the children who are living with leukemia, but their brothers and sisters, who often are puzzled, frightened, and left out in the cold while attention and love are lavished upon the sick child. Both schools of thought agree that it takes about a year after the death of the child for the stress to really hit the family. There is a potential for long-term survival in every victim, and some physicians think this should be the approach to the stricken family. What matters most is the openness of communication between all affected parties.

when someone dies

children and death

100 The death of a member of the family is part of a child's repertoire for coping with the world around him. The greatest shock of life for a child is death. Children adjust to death in a variety of interesting yet seemingly bizarre ways. For instance, after the death of a loved one a child will make some embarrassing identifications with the deceased. One child will start to call himself by his brother's name. Another will say he is the dead person. Now, it should be made clear that these identifications are not necessarily a part of every child's coping process. They are only possibilities. Sometimes children are so grieved that they will even try to mimic the state of unfeeling numbness associated with death. I know of one child who for some time was completely unhearing just as his dead brother was. And parents often impose the physical characteristics of the dead adult upon the children and will refer to the child's resemblance to the deceased. In their mourning, children adopt some disturbing behavior. It is normal and should be accepted by the adults in their lives.

For years adults kept the world of birth far from the eager ears and eyes of children. Today, even in families that pointedly oppose sex education, there is a greater openness about this once-taboo topic than ever before. But there is one subject still taboo in many homes and that is the concept of death and grief over death. Children are anxious about death. In fact, we could make an excellent case for death education being far more vital than birth education. There are those who would hush-hush any talk of death to children. Some families keep their children away from funerals as if they were the plague itself. Yet children worry about dying, and when loved ones die, they need to share some of the grief and some of the ceremony that surrounds this certain event. Isolating children at home during funeral times does little to help their normal anxiety. On the other hand, if hysterics are likely to be part of the scene, this would be bad for the developing child. Grief is the other side of the coin of love. Hiding grief from children gives them too partial a world. A reasonable sharing of death completes their circle of life.

odd names

making them responsible

When Shakespeare asked what's in a name, he wasn't familiar with studies that indicate that a child who is named Throckmorton or Guinevere is likely to have more mental health problems than one with a traditional name. Let's see how some of us name our children, why we thus name them, and then what is likely to happen. I am a good case in point. Having always been a devotee of the nineteenth century American author, Henry David Thoreau, who said, "A man is rich in proportion to the things he can do without," I have always harbored in the back of my mind the desire to name a son after Thoreau. So when my boy was born, I prevailed, and he was given Thoreau for a middle name. I haven't lived this down yet. Remember, a boy doesn't see the special significance of an odd name. A plain name virtually guarantees that the child will not face the jibes and kidding that those named Archibald do. Incidentally, not all strange first names produce personality problems. Strong personalities will not be affected, but at the age of a month or so, who can tell how strong a character a child will be?

When a parent can suffer the anger of a child to whom he has just said, "I care enough for you to force you to act responsibly," then that parent can rest assured that he is starting that child on the long road to responsible behavior. The worst thing that can happen to a child is to have a parent who never forces him to the responsible type of behavior. Just the other day I heard a story about two boys who used stolen money when they were only in grade school. The terrified boys went home and reported to their parents. One parent insisted that her boy return the money he used. As much as it hurt, as much as it embarrassed the child, it was the only responsible course for the parent to follow. The responsible parent acts responsible. For those who might see this as some signal to crack down on their children, let me caution that responsible behavior doesn't develop overnight in either parents or children. Be slow, be firm, and remember that children are learning; they aren't finished products.

just 'cause they're alive!

child abuse

I like the novel idea of Dr. William Homan who believes that children ought to be loved more frequently and shown more affection after they do nothing. Much is heard these days about reinforcing children's good behavior by attention and affection immediately after they do something that parents would like to see repeated again. For instance, if your child has just held the car door open for you, verbal or physical affection will make him want to repeat such action again. But children also need love and approval when they have done nothing in the way of accomplishment. An ice cream cone as a reward for a good arithmetic paper is very encouraging, but an ice cream cone just because you are you is the greatest! It is the celebration of what he is rather than what he does that makes a child flourish and feel good inside. Children are not performing puppies in a circus; they are not porpoises getting herrings for performance; they are human beings who need to feel approval just because they are alive. Continual rewarding of performance often leads to performance only for the reward, and often the price goes up rapidly.

There are children who suffer abuse and neglect without others realizing it. I was delighted to read a new American Humane Association brochure that helps school teachers and others to identify children who may be experiencing adult neglect. There are three areas to be observed in detecting neglect. The first is observations of the child's behavior, appearance, and attitudes: A child who comes to school too early may be a child who is pushed out of the home. An excessively withdrawn child or an unusually aggressive one may be telling us that things are not right at home. An undernourished, tired child also may be a clue. Obvious things such as welts and bruises that frequently appear and that are not easily explainable are a second sign of a child who is being beaten. Apathetic, unresponsive, or abusive parents are the third source of indicators that a child may need protection. School failure rarely comes from lack of ability. Most child abuse comes from parents who simply don't know better. All concerned adults need to be watchful.

shaking children

You are about to lose your temper and sock it to your little boy, and then you remember that physical punishment doesn't change behavior much. What do you decide to do instead of whamming him? Well, you shake the living daylights out of him—that's better than a beating, right? Wrong. Dr. John Caffey of Pittsburgh reports in the *American Journal of Diseases of Children* that shaking a child can cause severe injuries, broken bones, concussions, whiplash, brain damage, and even death. One nursemaid to middle-class children, whose folks thought they were hiring the best child-care possible, was blamed for killing three infants and injuring twelve others over an eight-year period. An infant's or child's head is very large for the relatively weak muscles in the neck that must support it. Violent shaking can burst blood vessels in the brain, and broken arms and legs can result from the shearing action of the shaking. Few who would think nothing of shaking a child would resort to a series of good punches to the head, yet the cumulative effect of shaking can be far worse than heavy blows to the head. Try squeezing, hugging, anything but shaking.

child labor

I thought that child labor in America was a memory from days gone by. If my neighborhood in middle-class America is any example, it is difficult to find a teenager willing to work for less than two dollars an hour. Nevertheless, there are some 800,000 child laborers on farms in our country today. Agriculture is our third most hazardous industry. The increasing use of poisonous chemicals and of complex machinery has made only mining and construction more dangerous. Here are some examples of children being abused. On a southern tobacco farm, twenty-three children between seven and fifteen were working in what amounted to an outdoor oven. In New York State children of fourteen were cleaning out barrels containing pesticides without adequate clothing for protection. Poor Mexican children laboring in Texas melon patches worked for forty cents a day. In some farming communities children put in ten-hour days alongside their parents who work for low wages. We need more farm inspectors and a more concerned citizenry.

103

loving behavior from our children

child's eye view of tv commercials

104

It isn't at all unusual for children to make sexual advances to their parents, who are the people they love. The correct reaction to a child caressing his mother's knee as she reads to him is not to become alarmed and think that she is dealing with some type of sick child, but to understand that behavior springs from affection. If the child persists in wanting to know why his mother will not allow this to continue, it is possible and therapeutic to say that this type of affection is reserved for the person you are going to marry. Incidentally, a male child may be as sexual with his father as he is with his mother. The only real danger is with the adult who, perhaps longing for such attention from a spouse, may unwittingly encourage the child by responding and not discouraging the behavior. Even the youngest of children will show this type of behavior. When my own daughter was fifteen, I can well remember receiving kisses from her that were obviously meant to be more than light pecks. A dismayed reaction would have hurt her feelings, but little response told her more than words or anger that her action was inappropriate.

Ann Kurth of Melbourne, Florida, testified before a Senate subcommittee on the effects of TV advertising. Miss Kurth is eleven and in the fifth grade. Ann has listened to commercials all of her life, and at times she has badgered her mother to buy this and that. When Ann's mom brought home a box of prepared cereal that had a record on the back of the box, the whole family was excited until they tried to make it work. It didn't. Little sister Martha, age seven, cried and was upset. Ann was angry. She decided to keep a record of commercials and also study their content. During a one-hour period of Saturday morning TV, she counted twenty-five commercial messages. When she extended her study of commercials to an hour of adult TV programs, she found that there were only ten or twelve. Here are some of her comments on commercials: Concerning an ad that says a particular cereal makes you feel groovy all day long, Ann says she tried it and didn't feel any different. A frozen dinner is supposed to have "fun" in it, and Ann says the commercial never says anything about the food. She concludes that "commercials would be good if they taught kids something that was true."

those cold cereals   tv violence, I

When, some months ago, Robert Choate attacked the manufacturers of the cold cereals consumed by the ton each year by American children, there were some sharp debates heard through the nation. A sidelight to this controversy recently brought to public attention was the fact that most of these cereals are sold on TV. Children's commercials on TV average twenty per hour, while the commercials on adult programs average twelve per hour. Half the children's ads are for food so that much of the child's attitudes towards diet and food are shaped in the more than 5,000 messages he receives on TV yearly. Food habits in America are already marginal, the nutritionists tell us, and this constant inundation of children by the manufacturers of candy and food held to be already seriously deficient in nutritive value only further deteriorates parental wisdom in this matter. That we are what we eat is nearly true. It is true enough to concern parents about what their children see and hear and stuff into their bodies.

In June 1968 an informal survey of eight hours of Saturday TV programming especially designed for children showed that there was unbridled violence — seven different kinds of pistols and revolvers, three varieties of rifles, three distinct brands of shotguns, half a dozen assorted daggers and stilettos, two types of machetes, one butcher's cleaver, an electric prodder, and a guillotine. The list is still longer. Men, women, and children were shot, burned at the stake, tortured over live coals, trussed and beaten by hoodlums, and lots more. At the end of eight hours anyone would be immune to the shock of seeing people hurt. Another survey, done a few weeks ago, indicated little or no change in program content. Pollution of the mind is as evil as air pollution. The only answer is for the public to sit down and write every buyer of commercial time on children's TV programs and protest. Send carbon copies to the FCC and your local station.

tv violence, II

violent tv produces violent children

106

There is a very clear relationship between violence on the TV screen and the subsequent aggressive behavior of children. The challenge of our time is the knowledge we need of how to master violence, how to find solutions to life's problems other than by shooting it out. Youth are living in the moments preceding the possible use of nuclear fission to destroy the world. On all sides of all oceans we see the development of armed camps. Our children, who will inherit this world, need to learn to abhor violence and to seek the ways of peace. They will never beat swords into plowshares who spend 16,000 hours in ten years before TV screens that preach doctrines of hate and violence. It is not good for children to see man any more inhuman that he naturally is. I see the distinct possibility of forcing stations to announce before most of the children's TV programs, "This program may be harmful to the mental health of your child." Let's clean up the air and the airwaves; they both can either enrich or pollute.

I suspect that the controversy over whether watching violent TV programs produces violence in children will continue for some time. Three specialists have just concluded a ten-year follow-up study of a group of third grade boys. Their summary states that heavy viewing of violent TV is linked with aggressive behavior in childhood and continued aggression in early and late adolescence. From what I can gather from this study by the New York State Department of Mental Health, these children, now age eighteen, have continued to show aggressive behavior ten years after they were initially studied. When children were asked to identify their classmates who were particularly aggressive, the latter turned out to be the very same ones who had watched much violent TV. The study began with 875 third graders who were studied at age thirteen and then at age eighteen. This is a large sample, and all the data in the first five years were upheld after the next five years. On the other hand, the surgeon general recently released figures indicating a mere tendency of children to imitate violence for a short period of time after watching violent TV. And so it goes...

giving back quality and culture

what's in the movies

Let's take a look at the arguments for and against TV commercials aimed at children. Opponents say that the commercials have an unfair advantage over the children in that they are highly persuasive with viewers who are unable to make independent evaluations of products. On the other side of the case, a poll found that three out of four adults approve the principle of commercial sponsorship of children's TV. Only 18 percent of adults objected to commercials for children, and of that percentage, 9 percent said that if the elimination of commercials means a decrease of programs for children, they would relinquish their stand. In other words, there is no significant groundswell of opposition to TV commercials aimed at the child watcher. A group called Action for Children's TV has just received a $164,000 grant to combat commercials for children. My own view: I do not want government control of TV, and I object to deceptive advertising in any form. A cleanup code would be feasible. Finally, I believe that no one ought to make money from children without giving back quality and culture.

A psychologist visited every movie playing in a moderate-sized American city in one week. After viewing thirty-seven films rated G to X, this is his statistical analysis: The average film contained thirty-eight incidents of violence and sex, including nudity, illicit sex, physical aggression, slaughter, and massacre. Sixty-two percent of the films presented dishonesty in a heroic light; 38 percent presented criminal activity as something that pays off and is an exciting pastime with no negative consequences. Forty-three percent of the films showed heroes as lawbreakers or as antisocial characters. In 59 percent the heroes killed one or more individuals. About half of the killings were presented as being justifiable. In 87 percent of the films the hero, whether antisocial or not, was portrayed appealingly. In 72 percent the hero's extramarital or promiscuous sex behavior was portrayed as normal and acceptable. Can this material affect developing children?

films can blunt emotions

violence and sex

If we consider that TV and movies can teach good things, exemplified in *Sesame Street,* and if we believe that films, such as the ones we show in schools or that we take our families to, can teach positive things, it seems possible that there are highly negative things learned too. Albert Bandura, psychologist at Stanford, has shown that children model their behavior after the things they see around them. Modeling or imitating is the way we learn what we believe. In other words, the film is a teacher of values. Indeed, because movies show life in full size and living color, it is quite probable that films are more instructive than parental admonition. There is some evidence that the recent spate of films that show in vivid detail killing after killing and that are preoccupied with debasing women and their bodies is very likely to lead developing humans into being emotionally blunted about violence and sex. The Church of Jesus Christ of Latter-day Saints counsels its members not to see any films rated X or R. Let's not bomb what we object to; let's exercise the option of attending or non-attending.

In the December 1971 issue of *Psychology Today,* Dr. Leonard Berkowitz makes some exciting statements about the issue of pornography and TV violence as it relates to both adults and children. He notes that on the one hand, the President's Commission on Violence has called for the end of such programs, while another commission has looked at pornography and concluded that its effects are harmless. The scientific investigations of both groups were excellent, and though both were fraught with inherent weaknesses, their conclusions brought strong yeses from the intellectual community. Yes, violence should be banned, and no, sex, known as pornography, need not be banned. Berkowitz, a professor at the University of Wisconsin, says that media violence does provoke aggressive reactions in viewers but only for a short time after viewing. Similarly, he argues, there are some viewers of erotic films who would behave somewhat differently, even violently, immediately after viewing pornography. Our society shuns violence, or so it seems, but it approves of sex. Can we have it both ways?

producing big leagues

little league as seen by the medics

Charles Bucher, at New York University, wisely counsels that in the elementary school years it is more important that a child's recreation be guided toward the fun of playing rather than winning, toward the child rather than the game, at the many rather than the few, toward informal activity rather than the formal, the development of skills in many activities rather than specializing in one. I think that all he has said makes sense, and I particularly aim my remarks today at those parents and coaches who have made little league just a shade less competitive than the big leagues. For all those who really think that they are producing little Vida Blues or McClains, let me remind them that Willy Mays once said he had never met a big leaguer that ever played little league. Big leaguers usually come from sand lot parks where there aren't fancy uniforms, or cleats, or screaming, rabid parents who think that there is nothing more to life than a successful ball game. A colleague of mine returned from a game the other night, and it seemed as if the world had ended. His son's team had lost by one run. Up to the age of twelve it doesn't matter. Life should be fun and not too earnest.

It seems, as the years go by, I become less and less rabid about certain subjects. In the past, I have frequently railed against nearly all forms of little league sports—baseball, football, and basketball. I still have serious reservations about youths between seven and twelve enjoying the totally structured team life these sports thrive on. So now I'll turn to some other professionals for their views of the super-competitive world of the little leagues. Fran Tarkenton, quarterback for the Minnesota Vikings, said, "I don't think boys of seven to twelve really enjoy playing in a structured situation. They do it today because all their friends are doing it; it's the thing to do, and no kid likes to be an oddball." Dr. Walter Char of Temple University Medical School said, "I shudder to think of the pressure put on some of these children when having to face a crowd of ten to 300 people." Dr. Nick Giannestros says, "Little league pitchers risk permanent elbow damage." Regarding midget league football Dr. Charles Cunningham stated, "Preteen youth are not anatomically ready for contact sports because the growing center at the end of their long bones is not yet solid." I still stand on my reservations.

little league dangers

competition in sports

110 Whitey Ford of the New York Yankees forbade his sons to pitch in little league baseball. He knew that when 160 boys aged nine to fourteen were X-rayed, all of the eighty pitchers had elbow malformations. This is a startling discovery. It wasn't, you will note, half of the group or two-thirds of them, but every single little league pitcher had elbow malformation. A regular pitcher in little league is destined to have chronic elbow trouble the rest of his life. It is only after the age of fifteen that the elbow is perfectly developed, and even then, who hasn't heard of tennis elbow? The act of pitching is not suited to the anatomy of the arm. It is a completely unnatural act for the bone structure, especially if a little guy has a knack for the curve or fast ball that demands a flip and twist of the wrist. This strains the so-called growth center of the elbow. Some men have suggested a sixty-pitch limit per game as one way of lessening the strain on a young elbow. A little league pitcher who pitches curves exclusively can kiss his arm goodbye. The art of real pitching had better wait till high school days, or Dad will never end up with a $100,000 bonus baby.

With the competitive sport scene already in full bloom for elementary and junior high school youngsters, it is particularly important for me to issue some warning to parents and coaches of teams that fight to the death for victories. A young child's self-esteem is often related to how well he pleases not only himself but his peers and the adults in his life. To be a failure in little league baseball, for example, can damage a child's progress in developing a strong self-image. His future may be seriously jeopardized by this area of failure. If your child must play league baseball or football, I would suggest that you become very aware of the importance of not attaching too much of his worth upon his sports prowess. In elementary school there is a great deal of poor coordination just because of the developmental period. The smooth playing that dads see on big league TV simply cannot be duplicated. Above all, competition is for the feeling of team spirit, for the enjoyable experience of winning and playing. Too much emphasis on personal achievement can damage the ego, and it isn't worth it.

what they don't like about adults

the corporate way and your family

When thousands of children across the country were asked what they thought of the adult world, here is what they said in *What Bothers Us About Grownups,* a report card on adults by children, published by the Stephen Green Press. Third graders said that it was adult noise, their screaming at you all the time, that most bothered them. In the fourth grade the children complained about adults talking too much, about bossiness, punishment, and rules. Ten- and eleven-year-olds are most bothered by the insults adults hurl at them in front of their peers. One child was disgusted with the invasion of his privacy and wrote on his questionnaire, "I this this is the silliest thing I ever heard of. Why do you ask such crazy questions?" I was interested to note that as early as a child's elementary school years he begins to make resolutions about what he will not say and do to his own children. Too many adults assume that childhood is a complacent time during which children are oblivious to adult behavior. In fact, children are always watching and comparing and ready to set the world right.

One of the more serious problems of our day is the mistaken notion that methods of solving problems faced by management in keeping track of material goods and production are equally good in the management of families, schools, and nonbusiness organizations. While it is true that people are people, it is also true that they function differently in their different environments. While performing before my college classes, I adopt certain techniques that are not applicable to my wife. At a meeting of a civic committee that I serve on, my behavior is still different. And with my tennis buddies I evidence some more varying patterns of behavior. Though in all cases I am trying to achieve certain results, my management of each unique situation cannot be identical. People aren't machines, nor are they cereal packages. And children aren't simply reactors to stimuli. Only sick or seriously retarded people need to be programmed to function creatively and effectively in their lives. Computers are great when used in their proper place at the proper time. Hail to thee, IBM cards, only manage not my heart.

family-life curricula

112 It has always seemed strange to me that in a nation where we have a soaring divorce rate and a great deal of marital unhappiness, we send most of our children through the schools with little or no study of human and family relations. While it may be true that knowledge alone doesn't make marriage or child rearing a guaranteed cinch, it is also true that a little know-how goes a long way when it is needed. Many parents are only biological parents, and they really haven't the remotest idea about what to do with real, live children. Many folks have little or no experience in learning how to settle an argument. It would seem that certain effective parents might be selected in communities to give the benefit of their experience. Most folks only need to sit around and work through their doubts and problems, except where there are extreme problems. But the schools should develop family-life curricula as an urgent matter. Waiting until marriage is accomplished and children are in the playpen is too little too late.

adolescence (13 to 22)

In 1967 when I wrote my first book, I included a section on adolescence, but I wasn't the parent of an adolescent then. I read what I was supposed to read and knew the research in the area, but I hadn't lived with one. I have now. I have four adolescents and a fifth who is not a blood member of the family. Much of what I wrote about adolescence before still holds true. I trust that the material you will read in this section bears the stamp of a greater authenticity than that which was found in *You and Your Child's World, Raising Fine Families,* and *Just a Minute.*

I have been tested in the crucible of adolescence, and the basic ground rules for parents as they live with adolescents seem to me to be essentially what I have said before. Nonetheless, there has been a certain leavening of my ideas, and this has come as a result of being the parent of adolescents.

Many professional journals are still filled with adolescent problems. Major textbooks talk about adolescents *ad infinitum.* In this volume I have chosen to consider the ages of eleven or twelve through twenty-one or twenty-two as the adolescent period in a person's life. Ordinarily this is divided into early adolescence, middle adolescence, and later

adolescence, so mixed into these many chapters are materials on early teenagers, middle teenagers and later teenagers. Thus, you shouldn't be too surprised to read about college students and even colleges in this particular section, while at the same time you will be reading about sixth, seventh, and eighth graders and, of course, high school students.

The turmoil of adolescence is practically uniform in the western world and already present in varying degrees in the eastern world. The adolescent is a person in search of himself, one who is preparing to separate from his parents prior to developing an intimate relationship with a member of the opposite sex.

Perhaps no other nation in the world is as preoccupied with its adolescents and their problems as are we in America. Very much a part of this section are numerous discussions about marijuana, heroin, hallucinogenic drugs, and the like. The reason for this is that in the search for identity, many of our young people, rather than face the developmental task, drop out of the struggle for independence and for the relationship between their parents and their own independence and enter into a world that, temporarily at least, precludes their

adolescence defined

attention to this very serious matter of growing up.

In the 1970s the American college and university have been much in the forefront. Starting with Kent State and that disastrous encounter between the public and the college students, and continuing through the various takeovers at Harvard, Columbia, and other prestigious institutions, the American public has become more and more concerned with and aware of the problems of the adolescent in institutions of higher learning. Inasmuch as I am a professor in one of those institutions, I have paid particular attention to adolescents on the collegiate level.

These words about adolescence come from Anna Freud. Whatever you may think of her father, you will hear some perceptive observations in this quotation: "It is normal for an adolescent to behave in an inconsistent and unpredictable manner; to fight his impulses and accept them; to love his parents and to hate them; to be deeply ashamed to acknowledge his mother before others, and unexpectedly to desire heart-to-heart talks with her; to thrive on imitation and identify with others, while searching unceasingly for his own identity; to be more idealistic, artistic, generous and unselfish than he ever will be again, but also the opposite: self-centered, egotistic, calculating. Such fluctuations between extreme opposites would be deemed highly abnormal at any other time of life. At this time, they signify no more than that an adult personality takes a long time to emerge, that the ego of the individual in question does not cease to experiment, and is in no hurry to close down on possibilities." If your teenager has seemed to be all of this and more, take heart. He's normal and struggling to achieve an identity of his own.

normal adolescence

when adolescents test

Most adolescents are normal in their growth. For them they are doing okay. Yet it is well to recognize that there is a great deal of anxiety in growing up. Children are preoccupied with being too short or too tall, too light or too heavy. This is natural, but they need to have their anxieties put to rest by information. Often an understanding pediatrician can assure a youngster that he may be, for the moment, too tall and out of joint but that he will go back into place as time goes by. Most adolescent girls worry about breast development. There really is no normal. Some girls start to bud at eight and some don't stop developing until they are nineteen. Most adolescents have acne problems, and nearly all of them can be helped somewhat by medical aid. I have found that if information that parents approve of is just left around, it will be devoured when the need arises. I think every home should have information about human growth and development available so the kids can consult it, albeit secretly, when they feel the need for knowledge. Only a few youngsters would not profit from books explaining normal development.

A favorite game adolescents play with their parents is to ask permission to do something that the youngster knows is wrong in the first place. When an eighteen-year-old asks a question that has an obvious answer both to him and to his parents, it is a sign that he is asking to be refused. A friend's daughter wanted permission to go out with a boy about whom a decision had been made a year earlier. He suddenly turned up, much to the chagrin of the adolescent. The girl in question knew full well that she did not want to go out with the young man — well, let's say she knew she shouldn't but still wanted to test the adult reaction to the idea. If it were positive or noncommittal, she might give it another try. When her parents said no, she remonstrated somewhat, but what red-blooded kid wouldn't? Her game was to see if her parents really meant to stay with a year-old decision. Adolescents are not always sure they are right or wrong. They need to feel adult values, especially when they vacillate.

what youth needs facing today

118 There is much flack these days from those who still feel that we coddle our youth instead of demanding conformity and obedience. The diary of a teenager in London who recently committed suicide gives thoughtful folks something to ponder. In her last note to humankind she said, "I'm just a dreamer, and none of my dreams will ever come true. I just can't face reality. I wish someone would really love me." It isn't good for people to feel like nobodies. Everyone needs to feel worthwhile. Of course, we don't know the circumstances behind this child's death, but it should prick us into considering the youth who surround us in our homes and neighborhoods. Just this day I had a colleague at the university tell me that his thirty-year-old son had never recovered from a teacher standing him before the class during his early adolescence, using him as an example of an obese child. Being unimportant forces people to live in fantasy worlds. If we live in these never-never lands long enough, we cannot, in fact, face reality. It is so easy to hurt the young with thoughtless jibes. Love isn't ever soft.

The author James Michener recently said, "It is more difficult to be a young person today than it was fifty years ago. What could happen to a young person in 1920? He could steal and find himself with a court record, or he could become a drunk, or he could contact a venereal disease, and that was about it. Today the young person is confronted by three new problems, each in its own way more destructive than the old: the draft, drugs, and worst of all, a general disaffection with life and alienation from our society." How true this is! I've thought much about yesterday and today, and I have no simple answers. At this point I really believe that if we had created a better, more honest and open world in the '20s, we would not be facing what stares at us today.

youth's goals   "into" things

If you think you have been falling behind in keeping up with the attitudes of the young, perhaps it is just as well. When I have used the term *generation gap*, I have prefixed it with the word *fabled* because I have often been persuaded that things are not as bad as they seem to be. Gilbert Youth Research in its 1970 survey of youth attitudes found that 54 percent of fourteen- to twenty-five-year-olds said that they would not report a known drug pusher. When only high school students were tallied, the percentage of those refusing to report a pusher rose to 66 percent. Sixty percent of these said that at least 50 percent of their friends used drugs. Only 12 percent of the ten- to twelve-year-olds named their mothers or fathers as the persons they most admired. Thirty-nine percent most admired a peer. Only 19 percent of elementary and high school pupils thought that the American way of life was superior to any other. Ninety-one percent said they would be willing to give a year of their lives to work for this nation to pursue a problem, and 42 percent of the youths said that their main goal in life is to make money.

One of the common expressions of certain members of the "with it" generation who are now seniors in high school or older is that they are one day "into" ecology, the next moment "into" pot, the next phase "into" civil rights, then "into" liberation, black power, or communes. The word *into* has been used to indicate that each one of these deep social concerns is a passing phase. How can you be into civil rights one year and out of it the next and then into communes and out of them for ecology? Adolescent minds are on the prowl for meaningful experiences, and it is not unusual for them to be flitting from one major social issue to the next. The philosopher Kierkegaard said, "Purity of heart is to will one thing." The ambulatory dedication of youth is not to be derided. The progression of their concerns is natural. Those who criticize youth who do not persevere in one area of human concern merely show their lack of real understanding of adolescence.

behavior is caused

homeyness

120 Some years ago we heard the idea that all behavior is caused. You know, I'm surprised at how frequently, in the past few years, the wisdom of the past has seemed to me to be so modern, so "with it," as the saying goes. Children who run away from home do so because of conditions that they consider to be intolerable. Children who don't go to school don't go because they do not find the events there to be stimulating. I am not commenting on the correctness of their assessment of either school or home; I am trying to point out that their behavior is caused. So when children continually behave abnormally, they are trying their best to cope with the life around them. In given stressful situations children achieve an easing of anxiety and stress by behavior often considered inappropriate in the adult world. Even though their bad behavior may produce some mighty uncomfortable results such as imprisonment or detention, getting rid of stress is more important than personal discomfort.

The other day I read where comedian-writer Sam Levenson said that a "homey" atmosphere cannot produce kids hooked on drugs. I think Sam was right. Too often we confuse homeyness with a good home that provides all that kids need to keep them occupied. Sam McLaughlin once said that circuses never keep children happy for very long. Sure, much of split-level America today provides minibikes, basketball courts, tennis lessons, and snowmobiles, but none of that can ever take the place of homeyness, which exudes a sense of more than love. It is the feeling that home is the place where, when you get there, they really want to take you in. As chairman of a citizens' advisory committee to a Utah juvenile court district, I have rarely heard a juvenile come before the court and tell us about how homey things were in the subdivision. If he does not demonstrate outright hostility toward his parents, he at least shows a basic rejection of all that home stands for. A house is not a home. Two parents living together don't necessarily add up to homeyness.

listening to youth   youth's inconsistencies

In May 1968, French students, along with workers, nearly paralyzed France with a revolt of gigantic proportions. In the family of Richard Jarville there was bitter contention. Simon Jarville felt that his children had gone beserk. They had long hair, argued incessantly, and were a vital part of the "events of May." This strict middle-class French family was nearly torn asunder until the mother, Simonne, age forty-seven, decided to find out what the revolt was all about. She traveled to the Left Bank of Paris and started to listen to her children's contemporaries. She learned that her children had some definite ideas about the very repressive school world in which they lived. Now five years later the Jarvilles say this: Children and parents should not only talk but listen to each other and be slow to judge. Rigid rules only create resentment. The control French families have on their children has always been legendary, but for many people like the Jarvilles, that is in the past. In many ways the liberation of French youth is quite exciting. Now in high schools the abject prostration before teachers has given way. The events of May have changed things forever.

One of the most insightful commentaries upon youth today comes from a column by James Reston in the *New York Times*. He reminds us that youth graduating from college today were born several years after World War II. They were in grade school when John Kennedy campaigned for the Presidency, teenagers when the war started in Vietnam. In their time of active memory, they have known only unrelieved turmoil, change, confusion, doubt, and temptation. They talk of commitment but do not commit themselves. They are full of energy but also full of intellectual slackness and laziness. They talk of wanting to participate in democracy, but they don't. They complain about a loss of individualism, and they run in packs. They condemn the welfare state but lean on it. So maybe, Reston continues, this new generation is not so different after all. They are our children with our own features, yearnings, and hypocrisies, only they are more visible, vocal, and open about expressing the tangles of life.

do we need youth?

the mediating adult

Until quite recently the Soviet Union kept statistics about teenage crime pretty well under wraps. Crime, the Soviets have always said, is the result of a decadent, capitalistic society. A teenage gang was caught after a spree of petty thefts, ending with murder. The reasons: "My life was in a fog," said one. "I was bored." This lad said that his family lacked nothing. They were comfortable by Soviet standards. Next to being bored, other youths claimed they wanted a thrill. And so it goes. Whenever a society emerges from its primitive state when it needs everyone to put his shoulder to the wheel, the life of ease and tranquillity breeds boredom. One of the real facts of modern American life is that there is no longer any need for youth. There was a time when young people were an integral part of everyday survival. It is all past now, and with no frontiers left, both young and old need to be diverted. Let's hope they don't bring lions and gladiators back.

In our town when school started last fall, there was anxiety for nearly everyone, especially for our teenager going into the great big high school. What is the role of a parent in dealing with his adolescent's fears? Let me quote Dr. Eli Bower, past president of the American of the American Orthopsychiatric Association. He said, "A family, or reasonable facsimile, exists to provide children with the best chance of experiencing a mediating adult. Such an adult is able to lower and connect affective bridges with children over which all kinds of cognitive-affective traffic can pass." Let me translate for you lest the psychiatric jargon throw you a block. All this says is that when children have either emotional or intellectual barriers to cross, the adults in his family can provide the means to comprehend and feel the experiences the child is going through. This is known as the mediating parent, and it is precisely why teenagers are generally not fit models for parenthood. If you can't understand your own ways, however will you mediate for a child?

how we see ourselves

peer pressure

123

What a person believes about himself may break him. I know of a case in which a youngster entering college was told that he was in the 98th percentile on the entrance test. He thought this meant that he had an I.Q. of 98, and so, seeing himself as only average, he predicted that college was going to be tough. He almost failed in his first semester. When he returned home for vacation, he told his parents he was a failure. They took him to a high school counselor who explained that being in the 98th percentile meant that only 2 percent of the entering class were brighter than he. Thus he was, in effect, about the brightest person in the freshman class. When he discovered that he was very bright, he returned to school and did excellent work. What we think of ourselves can doom or make us. An error in a technical explanation really didn't change his brainpower; it changed his view of himself. Our self-concept provides a screen through which we filter everything in our world.

What appears to be a revolt against the life-style of the establishment is most frequently a bowing to the pressure of a peer group. Dr. Fritz Redl once said that we have few real individuals among our youth. What we do have is a slavish dependence on the peer group code. Going along with the crowd is by no means a new phenomenon among either young people or adults. The common expression "keeping up with the Joneses" is applied to adults who will go to extremes to be like the next fellow. In classrooms a great deal of aggressive behavior is exhibited. This should not be construed necessarily as defiance against the teacher. Rather it may very well be the ritual of the puppet being manipulated by strings that are solidly attached to peers. The usual teacher reaction to surliness is to send the child from the room. It is vital that the message sent by the teacher read, "We want *you* in here; we don't want your behavior." Children who are confident of their capacities do not need to take their cues from peers as much as do those whose sense of self is grossly deficient. Genuine rebels are really those who are strong enough to resist meeting with everyone's approval.

runaway youth

why adolescents run

124 In the next year more than a million children will run away from their homes. They will leave behind guilt-ridden parents who will spend countless dollars and hours in futile searches. Most runaways end up on the street where they often fall victim to drugs, prostitution, and criminal avenues of escape. I believe all behavior is caused, and so I'd say that there isn't a child who leaves home who doesn't feel quite justified in his illegal behavior. But the streets are no place for little guys and gals in America, and so the organization known as Voyage, founded by the Reverend Jim Littrell in Philadelphia, is a welcome voice in the utter despair that running away creates. Voyage takes runaways into a home with a minimal, noncoercive atmosphere and puts them in close contact with peers who have already conquered their runaway problems. Voyage replaces the street, which most runaways finally conclude is not the ideal, free place they thought it would be. The adolescents' persistent search for the meaning of self is never satisfied in the jungle of the cities. It takes compassionate nonparents to create a place where these children can start to find themselves.

One of the pressing problems police and parents face, especially during the summer, is the runaway teenager. A youth conference on runaways held recently cited the fact that teenagers often flee home for the same reasons and fantasies their parents take trips and vacations. Wanting to escape the boring comforts of middle-class life is not unusual. After all, it is only the middle class that has the means to devise such absurdities as wife-swapping and one-shot marathon sensitivity sessions, so why be surprised that the children want a change of pace? Parents are justifiably puzzled when they find that their teenager doesn't enjoy taking a vacation with them, and they want to know why. The answer is really simple. One eighteen-year-old at the conference said, "We just don't want our parents breathing down our necks." In other words, youth respond to the same pressures parents feel, only they can't take a vacation, so they run away. Two problems that especially irk teenagers are the overstress on drugs and the lack of real communication at home. Is this agreed upon by everyone? You can't run away from reality.

the flower children

when adolescents revolt

I'm not at all sure I really remember what the word *hippie* means. It seems that oh so long ago that was all we heard from San Francisco to Atlanta. Where are they now, those youth whom Webster defined as a young person who rejects the mores of established society, dresses and behaves unconventionally, adheres to a nonviolent ethic, and prefers the use of psychedelic drugs or marijuana to alcohol? A survey recently found that in a western state only one out of four adults failed to paint a negative picture of the hippie. But today they seem to be gone. They did not develop a society that was nonviolent; indeed, the violence to health and sanitation they perpetrated is nearly beyond belief. As for their use of psychedelic drugs to blot out the reality of the society they abhorred, there seems to be some evidence that our adult drunkenness, never to be condoned, is nearly as serious a violation of the laws of health. The flower children are gone; much of what they abhorred still plagues the land.

An unusual and very perceptive explanation of adolescence may be found in the brilliant work of Erik Erikson reported in his book called *Childhood and Society.* He says, "In their search for a new sense of continuity and sameness, adolescents have to refight many of the battles of earlier years, even though to do so they must artificially appoint perfectly well-meaning people to play the role of adversaries; and they are ever-ready to install lasting idols and ideals as guardians of a final identity." I think this explains much that aggravates parents about their adolescents. When we constantly demand that they grow up and become something — and we do — and when they finally begin to act independently and grown up, they are chastized for their erratic, defiant, and independent attitudes. The old idea of childhood being made up of fixed stages is erroneous. Even at forty we fight again the battles of early childhood and of adolescence. The only real difference is that we are older and have to fight the battle ourselves. No one likes constraint, and everyone wants and needs it. Boy, chimps have it easy!

why drugs

126 The Child Study Association's pamphlet called *You, Your Child and Drugs* has done the adult community a great service. This mighty little pamphlet points out that drug misuse is a process — a chain of events that takes a while to happen. Usually it is peer pressure that gets a youngster started, and this is often a one-time dare. But when certain other conditions prevail, it isn't too difficult to see that taking drugs becomes a way out, a way out of tension and boredom, both of which are normal concomitants of adolescence. They become a way out of parental control and a way out of any form of authority, a way out of despair such as that which is caused by academic failure and, curiously enough, academic success. The school rat race can often lead to such despair. There is no one cause for taking drugs. If anything comes close to it, it is the deprivation theory that says that when youngsters feel severely deprived of anything, they turn to whatever will blot out the deprivation. They don't need everything they want but do need a little of what every human craves — a feeling of significance at home, in school, and around the neighborhood.

Drugs have been a concern now for some years. The treatment of youngsters on drugs is beset with problems both ethical and scientific. On the one hand, we have arguments about the truthfulness of research data that seem to conclude at one time that there are harmful effects and at others that, with the exception of heroin, many drugs don't seem to be any more potent than alcohol. When a drug such as methadone is substituted for heroin, there are cries about the idiocy of using one drug to reduce the desire for another. Whichever way the data finally go, society is still plagued with the terrifying problem of young people behaving like cabbages in a world crying for them to tackle its problems. These are the youth who are immobilized by drugs, by alcoholism, or by serious mental problems that paralyze the mind and stunt human development.

how to tell if they're on drugs

who'll become an addict?

Although there seem to be some hopeful signs that our drug problem is receding somewhat, it is still important that parents be on the alert for the most common signs that show a youngster is on drugs. When a child is on heroin or opium, there is often a drastic loss of weight. When on heroin, morphine, or codeine, there is a continually running nose. When glue sniffing fills his spare moments, there is a general redness and a watering of the eyes. When amphetamines are used, there is a constant licking of the lips, finally resulting in chapped lips. When cocaine is sniffed, there are red, raw nostrils. When heroin is used, the kids usually wear long sleeves to hide needle tracks. In all cases of suspicion the parent needs to watch for personality changes. Good students start to fail, extroverted kids become sullen, and introverted ones often become noisy. One of my students at the university said something interesting the other day. Today any kid who gets hooked has only himself to blame. Everyone knows it's a bad deal all around.

Dr. John Ives, professor of psychiatry at the University of Vermont and a physician who served in Vietnam during the heroin epidemic of 1970-72, reports some facts that echo some of my past sentiments. As he examined the backgrounds of these addicted men, he invariably found that the family history included divorce and separation, poor relationships between the addict and his parents, and the use of alcohol or tranquilizers by those parents. The addict himself had invariable dropped out of high school, mostly for disciplinary reasons rather than academic ones, and he had often had difficulty finding and holding a job. He had usually enlisted in the army in order to get away from home or to avoid a jail sentence, or else he really didn't know why he had enlisted. It was also found that the addict in the army had rarely taken any drugs prior to his service. So what does all of this add up to? To me it says that it shouldn't be too difficult for schools to make some pretty good guesses about potential drug users and then to develop rapport with such students so that they succeed in school and feel good about themselves, good enough so that they don't need to turn to drugs for comfort.

some new drugs   speeding toward trouble

Although it is true that the use of heroin has dropped in American cities, its place has been taken by a rash of new drugs that are mind-altering and horribly dangerous. In many cities a drug called methaqualone is being used along with methadone. But there are some interesting reasons for the drop in heroin usage that seem to me to augur well for an eventual decline in the misuse of all drugs. Somehow word is out among the youth that it is no longer cool to be a junkie. In fact, junkies are considered sick. Another reason for the drop is the large-scale treatment programs that have taken thousands of addicts out of circulation and, unfortunately, put too many of them on methadone, which has now become the street drug that heroin once was. The most terrifying thing now is the widespread use of barbiturates, which are addictive and more dangerous than opiates. Barbiturate withdrawal kills; opiate withdrawal seldom does.

Amphetamines are the little pills that have for years depressed the appetites of overweight people. They are also the little pills that give a real high to those who don't need to lose weight. In fact, up to as much as 50 percent of amphetamine production has been diverted to the black market where it eventually becomes known as speed to thousands of young people now commonly called speed freaks. The initial effect of speed in modest quantities is to perk up mental and physical energy, while larger doses lead to an exaggerated euphoria accompanied by a sense of unlimited power. Dissolved in water and injected in the vein, the powdery substance produces a "rush," which is an immediate sense of uncontrollable elation of mind and spirit. In two or three hours this wears off, and there is a terrible urge to shoot up again. Since the body develops a tolerance, the dosage has to be continually increased. Thank goodness federal law is now cutting production drastically and there will be fewer maimed young minds.

the drugs we use

heroin?
just
a habit!

The National Commission on Marijuana and Drug Abuse has reported that America's third most popular drug after alcohol and tobacco is marijuana. Thirteen million Americans consider themselves users of marijuana. There are 80 million drinkers and 57 million tobacco smokers. There is also ample evidence that millions of Americans have tried even stronger drugs than any of these three. Here are some really interesting facts: Over 80 million people had consumed an alcoholic beverage one week before the survey. This figure means that 24 percent of all American youths and 53 percent of all adults had a drink one week prior to the survey. While not regular users, 25.9 million people have tried marijuana, including 14 percent of all youths and 16 percent of all adults. Almost 4.8 million people have tried cocaine, 2 million have tried heroin, and 7.6 million have tried LSD. America, it seems, is its own worst enemy. I shudder to think of these figures in 1980.

I don't know when I have been more dismayed and shocked by any remark than the one made by Ira Glasser, executive director of the New York Civil Liberties Union. He said, "Taking heroin is logically and philosophically indistinguishable from smoking, drinking, overeating, and a whole lot of other bad habits." He goes on to say that the number of heroin addicts is far smaller than the number of smokers or alcoholics. He finally concludes that heroin ought to be made available in pharmacies for addicts. It is entirely inconceivable to me for someone to call heroin addiction just another bad habit. You can't just dabble with heroin—take it now and again the way alcohol is used. Most addicts claim they were sure they would never get hooked. Most users of alcohol and tobacco don't become alcoholics or nicotine fiends and find themselves stealing to obtain enough money to maintain a habit. There are no alcohol junkies. No one furtively sells cigarettes on street corners. If I have ever heard an irresponsible, extremist pronouncement, this one takes the prize. Heroin just another habit? Not on your life.

marijuana and the brain

marijuana and alcohol

marijuana and alcohol

130

I have never known information to make very much difference to the way people regulate their lives. I have heard that the only way to make rational decisions is upon fact, not theory, not idiosyncrasy, but cold, hard data. Yet millions drink the deadliest of drugs—alcohol. There are millions who don't buckle up seat belts. So I expect that this letter about marijuana from six professors of medicine at the College of Physicians and Surgeons at Columbia University won't phase anyone either. They say: "Marijuana contains toxic substances that are stored in the brain. Moderate usage is difficult to achieve because we develop a tolerance to cannabis, which means we have to increase the dosage to obtain the initial effect. As a result, marijuana users are likely to need stronger stuff, perhaps hashish, or to escalate to more potent drugs." They go on to say that marijuana induces cancer in tissue cultures of human lungs. It also leads to cellular damage in man. Man's immune response of his white blood cells is impaired in marijuana users.

The controversy over marijuana is not likely to end tomorrow morning. As a nation we do not punish those caught possessing a substance such as alcohol that is a central nervous system depressant and that has produced a physical dependence in better than six million people and a psychological dependence in probably thirty million others. But we do punish those who possess and use marijuana, which is not likely to produce psychological of physical dependence. It is a mild hallucinogen, and for its possession you can get ninety-nine years in some place. Our young really do scoff when they see their parents with their senses dulled behind the wheels of powerful engines that kill thousands yearly, while what youth term harmless reveries with marijuana do nothing of the kind. Legalization of this drug is, to my mind, a foolhardy attempt to allow two wrongs. Marijuana delays the growing-up process in the young because it takes the child from the arena of conflict so essential to the growth process.

aftermaths of marijuana

why kids quit grass

A few years ago Dr. Harvey Powelson, chief of the Department of Psychiatry, Student Health Service, at the University of California at Berkeley, said that marijuana should be legalized and controlled. Since then his experience with persistent marijuana users has led him to reverse his earlier feelings, and now he states the following: "The use of marijuana leads acutely—and for several hours to days thereafter—to a disorder of thinking characterized by lack of coherence and an aggravation of pathological thinking processes. The effects of marijuana are cumulative, and after a period of prolonged use, meaning six months to a year, and frequent dosages, such as one joint per day, chronic changes occur that are similar to those seen in organic brain disease, that is, patches of lucidity amid areas of fogginess." Where marijuana is heavily used, the students who drop out of school because of its usage can't resume their studies because they are unable to think clearly and seem to have lost the will to do anything that requires much effort.

Victor Perera, who teaches at the University of California at Santa Cruz, a school that has the reputation for being a "doper's" campus and the largest major drug outlet in northern California, has just written about a frank discussion he had with nineteen students in his class concerning marijuana. Of the nineteen, six admitted smoking pot heavily, three had never smoked, six were former smokers who had given up dope entirely, and four were phasing it out. Most were giving up the grass because it was too expensive. I was interested in some of the reasons others stopped indulging. One student quit because he wanted to be in control of himself. One said, "I'm too curious. I'm deeply involved with my energies. Music excites and energizes me. Dope is a bring-down. I hardly ever mess with it any more." One said she finds it too undignified. "When I smoke I get all giggly and silly, unable to control my speech. Afterwards I feel like an absolute idiot." Another gave it up because it reduces all experiences to the same level.

what methadone does

methadone and heroin

Methadone has too often been seen as the panacea for curing the thefts or rip-offs that addicts must engage in in order to support their habits. Methadone is a substitute for heroin. Methadone is less costly and more deadly in many ways. It is deadly because it kills. Methadone overdose is not too unusual nowadays since it has become the backbone of many programs that rely on it instead of on changing behavior. Dr. Carl Zelson of New York Medical College has reported that infants born to mothers taking methadone have more severe reactions to the drug than heroin-addicted babies have to heroin. Interestingly, the severity of the infant's withdrawal symptoms is not related to how high the dosage is as it is in heroin-addicted infants. In a study of forty-six babies born to methadone-addicted mothers and forty-five infants born to heroin-addicted mothers, twenty of the methadone babies required treatment for withdrawal, and only six of the heroin babies needed similar treatment. Methadone causes babies to be born underweight, some with hyaline membrane disease, and others with seizures and jaundice.

I have been accused of being against methadone maintenance programs for the treatment of heroin addiction. I have also been accused of being terribly pro the therapeutic, psychiatrically oriented community. I shall define them (both of these terms explain my stance on both modes of the treatment of drug addiction, let the chips fall where they may): Methadone treatment is the use of the drug methadone to serve as a substitute for heroin. Methadone addicts people to it. When taken in doses not prescribed, it is a lethal killer, worse than heroin, in fact. Methadone programs usually, but not always, provide counseling for addicts so that they may eventually become totally drug free. Most addicts on methadone never become drug free. They simply use methadone along with nearly everything else. The therapeutic community is a completely drug-free approach; it is difficult and most often results in failure except for a few who do surivive its rigors and move back to the normal community. Neither approach is dramatically successful. Kicking drugs is difficult.

lsd   a new low

With all the talk about hallucinogenic drugs, it might be well to review some of the facts about the principal mind-altering drug known as LSD. Our pill-oriented society today has finally begun to realize that all is not well with the youth of the land who have turned away from the values of this society and, instead of attempting to do something, have turned to drugs that plug them into flights of fancy. What about LSD? An average dose the size of a speck of salt lasts from eight to ten hours. It is strange but true that conflicting feelings often coexist in the user after he takes the drug; that is, he is sad and happy or relaxed and tense at the same time. No evidence indicates that there is any increase in creativity, but rather there is panic after a trip, and paranoia, which makes the user suspicious of people for up to seventy hours after using the drug; and there is a chance of recurrence for days, weeks, and months after use. Those who indulge in hopes of escape may indeed get out of this world for awhile, but the reentry is frightening and frequently terrifying, and worst of all, the user is right back where he started.

When the drug industry goes merrily on its way producing 147 million 300-milligram pills of a new drug called methaqualone, you can bet that the drug sub-culture of this nation, too often aided and abetted by chic adults, will discover the supply and rip off what they can. And they have. Methaqualone is a nonbarbiturate depressant introduced in this country in 1965. Initially it was a sleeping pill with fewer addictive characteristics than barbiturates. In hip language, using the drug is called "doing sopors" or getting "ludded out." It has been called the heroin for lovers because it is supposed to lower sexual inhibitions. Its action mimics a heavy drunk with none of the gastrointestinal complications. It is also used mostly in combination with alcohol because meth-aqualone has a synergistic or enhancing effect upon alcohol. Fortunately youth are learning that it is terrible addicting, expensive, and boring. Withdrawal after addiction is rather fierce; near fatal overdoses are an easy mistake to make, and when you are hooked, it is nearly impossible to withdraw.

drugs and pregnancy

drugs in the schools

134 A study of middle- and upper-class women in Houston, Texas, disclosed that each woman used an average of ten different drugs during pregnancy, with a range of from three to twenty-nine. One intelligent mother took twenty-five aspirin tablets a day throughout her pregnancy because she always did. She said she never would have had she known aspirin is a drug. In this same Houston study 41 percent of the women took antibiotics during pregnancy, 35 percent took anti-acid preparations, and 13 percent smoked a pack of cigarettes or more, thereby exposing the fetus to large amounts of the drug nicotine. The same study showed that while mothers-to-be self-medicated themselves heavily, the danger from doctors' prescriptions was worse. For example, a recent study of 911 women in Scotland showed that excluding iron, drugs of some type were prescribed for 82 percent of the women, with an average of four drugs prescribed per woman. The best advice is for pregnant women to say no to any drugs over which they have control.

It was a shock for New Yorkers to discover what I experienced while teaching in the East Bronx twenty years ago—that in many schools there is wholesale drug use and sales. In some New York City schools 90 percent of the students are on drugs of some sort. Last year there were 7,783 known users of heroin. It is generally conceded that whenever we have any known figure, we can reliably double it to get the actual number of cases. Nearly 60,000 students were known or suspected of using various hard and soft drugs. I shall never forget the incredulous look on my principal's face when he discovered that there was planted in our own junior school in 1952, not 1972, a federal narcotics agent who saw drugs sold, slipped, and used openly. Even at that time there wasn't anyone who didn't know who the pusher for Junior High School 52 was. He roamed the halls unmolested, sporting $100 suits and passing out cigars to teachers. The most important question each of us can ask is, what is the true extent of drug use in our schools?

drugs and dependence

drug-free treatment

Those who used to be called hippies are now called world travelers. In Kabul, Afghanistan, American world travelers can still live on a dollar a day, including hashish. Four to five thousand Americans are there now, and they are not idolized by the Moslem community. One twenty-five-year-old girl from Connecticut said, "The kids are just lost and killing themselves, and probably the worst thing is, they stop responding." One of the inevitable results of continued drug usage is the feeling that nothing counts, nothing is too important —not life, not anything. I spend a share of my time among addicts. I can attest to the complete dependence the adolescent has on a substance such as cannabis or hashish to pull him up by his bootstraps. The underlying message in the youth revolt of the 1960s was that man had become too far removed from his fellowman. Certainly dropping out of the entire human scene through the use of drugs isn't any cogent answer to their criticism. There are alternatives to drugging oneself insensible. People in trouble can get help. All they need do is call Project Reality, Odyssey House, Daytop, or Synanon wherever they are. Help is often just a phone call away.

Odyssey House is a free rehabilitation center with residential treatment facilities. It is a no-nonsense approach to adolescents and others with either drug or other types of disabling problems that require intensive, long-term supervision. I am very impressed with the aims and methods of Odyssey House because it recognizes that people with drug or alcohol problems need more than pity, apathy, or disgust. Usually they are people who think so little of themselves that they drown their misery in these not-so-gentle persuaders. There are three phases of treatment in the Odyssey House program: induction, conducted by ex-addicts and professionals, is designed to motivate the street addict into wanting to enter into a therapeutic relationship with others; the treatment phase is a reconstruction of the addict's personality and can take as long as eighteen months; reentry into the real world, the third phase, is where the addict charts his vocational course. The basic concept of the program is open confrontation with one's self through the eyes of others like one's self.

teaching the young about drugs

turning on to smoking

136

Recently we learned of the failure of a drug education program in Michigan. As a result of the program, usage increased instead of decreased. Let me give you an example of how the truth can decrease fears and thus lead to more experimentation on the part of seventh graders. For some time now even professionals have gone around with the idea that withdrawal from heroin causes hours of untold anxiety, agony, and the most violent kind of symptoms. Yet in my experiences at Odyssey House, a drug-free therapeutic community, I have never heard or seen a single heroin addict crashing in the manner described in movies and books. When kids discover that withdrawal doesn't mean crawling the walls, it is possible, is it not, to hear them saying, "Well then, it can't be so bad." It is not the physical effects or noneffects of drugs that need to be emphasized in drug education programs. Children need to feel how dependent it makes one—how out-of-it they become, how babylike they act. The loss of humanity is what counts, not the malnutrition that may not appear.

If you have $15,000 you don't know what to do with, but you are anxious to support an almost sure-fire way to stop smoking among teenagers, then send your money to Dr. Eugene Levitt at Indiana University, because I believe he has a large part of the answer. Dr. Levitt studied 50,000 Indianapolis teenagers and their smoking behavior and came up with these results: If a teenager's best friend smoked, then he smoked. The relationship between one's teenage friends smoking and the smoking habits of teenagers was so overwhelming that Levitt has devised a superb plan. Some tactics might be employed. For instance, girls could refuse to date smoking boys, or bonfires could be staged where all smokers throw their packs into the bonfire at once. Dr. Levitt has some of the keys because he knows that movies and adult-inspired speeches and testimonials don't make much of a difference.

school counselors

what a behaviorist does

High school counselors can be important people in the lives of adolescents. When counselors were asked in a recent study what they did all day, the replies indicated that they were kept busy: they filled out job and college applications, truancy reports, curricula change forms, honor rolls, grade lists, and a host of things that any clerk could do. The study, titled "Career Guidance: Who Needs It, Who Provides It, Who Can Improve It," included thousands of counselors and concluded that no amount of screening has filtered out emotional misfits. This is important because it is not uncommon to have maladjusted persons enter the various helping professions in a search for answers to their own lives. There are occasions when poor teachers are counseled into counseling, thus providing an opportunity to fill their slots with good teachers. The study showed that the training of counselors is often only academic, giving little opportunity for on-the-job training. Finally, there is evidence that counselors tend to shy away from the real problem cases, feeling a certain anxiety about dealing with a severe emotional difficulty for which they are not trained.

In all fairness to my friends who are behavioral psychologists, I should again explain what it is they do that differs so markedly from the traditional psychiatric approach. Let us assume the hypothetical situation of a mother coming into a child-guidance clinic and complaining that she is having trouble with her fourteen-year-old son who is rebellious. Traditional approaches would often delve into the background of the case, trying to determine what there was in the child's experiences that may have caused this annoying behavior. The beharioral therapist is not much interested in the why of things. His major concern is with an accurate description of the exact nature of the behavior. That is, he wants to know what precise behavior is causing mother trouble and how often that behavior occurs in a week. Indeed, he will, in all likelihood, send the mother back to her home with specific instructions to keep an accurate record of the frequency with which a certain behavior occurs. Then both can work on reducing the number of times this behavior happens. And so the treatment progresses.

absent from school with permission

when children err

The time has come to get rid of the anachronism of the average daily attendance as being the way states reimburse districts for part of their educational expenses. It isn't, and it never has been, the factor of absolute attendance that determines success in school. Now there is a difference between attendance and truancy, and that is not what we are talking about. Let me tell you about a fascinating experiment of Olympic High School in Charlotte, North Carolina. There upper-classmen were allowed fifteen excuses from class, with no explanations necessary until the sixteenth absence. After the sixteenth absence, the student was automatically denied credit. In addition, students were fully responsible for all work missed during the no-excuses-necessary days. Interestingly enough, attendance went up, not down, and the paperwork done by the school decreased visibly. Also, for nearly the first time in the school's history, there were no suspensions for truancy. It seems as though folks will do almost anything to get around rules and regulations. Some sharp attention to this proposal, modified or not, deserves the time of school officials.

One of the reasons Americans sort of hang their heads over the statistics on juvenile delinquency is because we count a host of things as offenses that no one else considers. In most countries of the world, a child is brought to court only if he commits an offense that would be considered a crime if an adult did it. So it isn't too difficult to see that truancy, stubbornness, leaving home, curfew violations, and offenses of that nature swell our delinquency picture and make us appear to be far more deliquent than our neighbors. What has happened in this country is that we have, in our desire to afford greater protection to youth, covered a multitude of sins with our laws. Thus, while in many ways we do protect children more, we also look pretty barbarous even to ourselves. Our figures concerning adult laws broken by juveniles is pretty serious in and of itself, but when you throw in ungovernability and smoking, it adds up to a pretty dismal picture. We might do well to consider still maintaining our vigil over truancy and the like but not recording and reporting it as a juvenile offense.

who's delinquent?

gangs of the 1970s

Researchers in Illinois asked 3,100 youngsters aged fourteen to eighteen to tell whether they had engaged in any of thirty-five delinquent behaviors. Contrary to long-held assumptions, juvenile delinquency was nearly as widespread among girls as boys. For each of the thirty-five delinquent behaviors identified, girls reported a much higher delinquency rate than official records led the scientists to expect. The only finding that squared with theory was that the adolescent girl was somewhat less delinquent than were boys of the same age. Delinquent behavior occurs almost equally among black and white, rich and poor, urban and rural youngsters. These findings challenge the assumption that delinquency occurs more often among males in urban slums. The reason we hold this assumption is because the male slum dweller is more likely to get arrested than his counterpart by sex and by economic status. What do you think was the most common aberrant behavior? Seventy-three percent of the kids admitted to cheating on schoolwork. Next were drinking, making anonymous phone calls, petty thievery, and breaking and entering. Least frequent was using heroin.

The street gangs that died in the 1950s are back now with a vengeance, according to police in major cities. Back in the so-called good old days of the fifties, there were what was known as gang rumbles such as are sung about in *West Side Story*. Opposing gangs met in a park or under a bridge in a dark corner of town and they would fight it out. Not today. In an imitation of gangland techniques, gang leaders now resort to quick hits, using just two or three boys to zero in on one member of the opposing gang. Do you remember the day of the old-fashioned, homemade zip gun, which was a crude weapon that was just as likely to wound the shooter as the intended victim? Today handguns of every variety, grenades, bazookas, and rifles are the usual weapon. The gang fights are touched off just as they were in old days—by territory and women. In Los Angeles last year the death toll from gang wars was 32; in Philadelphia ninety-two lives have been claimed in the last three years. The reason for this resurgence—hordes of slum dwellers with little to do but look for trouble, they have no place to go, no place to work.

rat packs

violent films

140

A medical student and his companions are on their way home from a hard week at the Mount Sinai College of Medicine in New York City. Suddenly three youths approach them and ask for a quarter. The medical student walks on paying no attention since he doesn't have a cent on him. Suddenly a shot rings out, and he is lying on the street, a bullet in his back near the spine. And so it goes in some of the larger cities of America where what is called rat packs, or groups of three or four slum youths, wander about begging and often committing violence if they don't get what they want. These children are of junior high and high school age and are no longer in what many of us knew as organized gangs. Those days are gone forever. Whereas the gangs tended to just rumble with one another, these rip-off artists, as they are called, form small bands and harrass individuals who look like they have some money. When asked about how they see the future and the human race, it isn't at all unusual to hear that they don't think of a future and that they think the human race isn't much. Most of these children are poverty-stricken, come from home situations that are desperate, and have no heroes except the neighborhood riffraff.

We have accepted the principle of catharsis as a justification for passion and violence in the movies. There is no evidence, however, that after seeing a particularly violent film, we are more peaceful. Nearly all the evidence suggests the opposite. After seeing violence, we are more prone to violence. The same may be said about erotic, pornographic materials. They are touted as being cathartic by those who would foist everything under the sun before our children's eyes with the specious reasoning that it gets some of our sinful ideas out of our minds and out of the realm of action. Children today not only view murder, rape, and mayhem; they see the bullets passing through victims, they see heads literally blown off, and in the long run I suggest that they start to become immune to brutality. The nature of man is still more important in art than the realism of his demise.

shoplifting

no jails for youth

Not too many years ago the only time a child was alone in a department store was when he lost his parents. But times have indeed changed, and America's youngsters are now a part of the shopping set, that is, middle-class society that has found a way of life in aimless meanderings through the shopping malls in search of who knows what. It used to be that folks went to the store when they needed to buy something. Not so these days. People roam the malls seeking to develop needs they never dreamed they had. And so their children have learned that if there isn't anything to do—and there isn't much to do in suburban American—then a fine way to spend the day is sharing the walkways of the shopping plazas with their mothers. With nothing to do, no place to go, and tons of merchandise on display, young America is shoplifting everything in sight. Contributing more than a little to this delinquency is the present idea that ripping off the establishment is part of the good fight, and so a juvenile pastime has reached epidemic proportions.

There is startling news from Massachusetts concerning the new treatment of juvenile offenders. There are no longer any juvenile prisons in this state, and this is welcome news to many. It costs about $10,000 per year to keep a juvenile in jail in Massachusetts. This is enough money to send a child to Harvard and give him a $100-a-week allowance, a summer vacation in Europe, and once-a-week psychotherapy. Most juvenile specialists feel that state industrial schools and the like are wastes of time and money. It is a fact that 60 to 80 percent of those put into juvenile detention facilities for indeterminate periods of time are not rehabilitated and, indeed, return to jail. Further, in many state systems there is brutality on the parts of both those jailed and those who keep them. The list of objections to these prisons is very long. Does this mean that no offenses will be dealt with? For those who are really dangerous to society there are private provisions made to house them securely. The rest live in group homes, are paroled, or are given individual treatment programs.

before you take your child to court

retrieving failing students

All parents need to know what their children's right are if they are brought before a juvenile court. May I preface this report by trying to allay the fears of those who feel that I should not advertise these rights but emphasize the responsibilities of children and parents. I agree that responsibility is paramount, but not all children who go before juvenile judges are automatically guilty as charged. Therefore, all parents should know that under the laws of this land, these are your child's basic rights: First, he has the right to have due notice of the charges against him so that he doesn't have to appear before a judge and be surprised by his statements. Second, your child has the right to be represented by a lawyer, appointed by the court if necessary. Third, he has the right to confront and cross-examine witnesses and complainants. And finally, he has the right to not testify against himself and the right to remain silent. In other words, children have the same guaranteed constitutional rights as others in this society. Of course, there will be those who will use the law to cover up guilt, but this argument forgets that one purpose of the law is to make very certain that not one innocent person is unfairly dealt with.

There's more than one way to skin a cat, and there is more than one way to take a failing student in high school and put him back on the track. A young teacher in Connecticut has just received a massive grant to take low-achieving students into the wilderness where they may get lost in the terrain but usually find themselves. After all, student failure is rarely a matter of intellectual poverty. Most kids are bright enough to succeed in school. What causes most school failure is the paralysis caused by the total school – home – community environment that oppresses children who don't conform to the expected pattern. The less they conform, the more the pressure increases, and the inevitable tale of failure starts to evolve. The wilds, in some mysterious way, unleash potential and drain off energy that ordinarily would be used to taunt others and annoy teachers. When a child pits himself against mountains, storms, and rivers and succeeds, he starts to stand taller. I wonder when schools will wake up and realize that remedial holes in the wall, often called classrooms, don't really make much difference.

rights and responsibilities of 18-year-olds

the new morality: lonely adolescents

Now that America has amended the Constitution so that eighteen-year-olds can vote, there is a strong movement afoot to accord certain other rights to this portion of our population. I can remember way back in 1943, in the middle of World War II, a slogan that said, "If we are old enough to die, we are old enough to vote." Well, it took over twenty-five years for that early protest to catch the imagination of the public eye. There's some real sense in the idea. Look at it this way: Thousands of eighteen-year-olds are married, yet they can't make a will. Many cannot enter into certain financial agreements. At seventeen a person becomes an adult for criminal law purposes, yet he needs a guardian or co-signer for a $500 financial matter. A minor may earn money without guardian supervision, but a garage man cannot collect his bill from that same minor. And so it goes in hundreds of situations where present laws don't make sense. If they can vote, they deserve some of the liabilities. With independence comes responsibility.

In an article published in the New York Times, a black adolescent says to the writer: "I'll tell you the...big mistake you...make. You think it is easy to be young and just go running around, no cares, no responsibilities. That's your mistake. You all think we can do anything and get away with it, but that's because you're only interested in the excitement. You know something? They got girls in this school so lonely they can't talk about it. But when they get themselves pregnant, then someone's got to listen. Ain't nobody interested in a boy or girl...trying to figure our their lives, what they're gonna become, you know. But if he gets a girl pregnant or beats her up, then the adults come running." Somehow there is a certain degree of vulgar curiosity among adults for children in trouble. Then we want them to behave. Too much of society thinks that values come from films and books; too little, from parental example.

who invented the sex revolution?

who teaches sex?

A recent article has an interview with an adolescent that every adult needs to read: "You move with the times, man," says this nineteen-year-old, now on speed and acid. "People have expectations for you, so you live up to 'em. It's the same with you. Society's got a hold on your leg too. It says marry some chick and stay that way. Me, it says mess around and be a big man. Only thing I wish is that you guys would make up your mind about what we're supposed to do. You talked here the other month about a sex revolution. No kid my age is smart enough to invent something like that. Anything that big has gotta come from the old and the rich. So when you all make up your mind, we all might get it together down here. Till that time, man, I got lots of tears left to come out, and lots of pills." What *I* hear is a clear call for moral guidelines from elders. Despite a tradition of freedom in America, we have, in the name of civil rights, too often let the sewers wash our children.

I rarely answer mail that asks specific questions because it would be the height of folly for me to attempt to be specific with as little information as one receives in a letter. Besides, Ann Landers and Joyce Brothers don't need any assistance from me! But the letter I got the other day from a woman in Seattle cries for some response, She claims that her husband has not instructed her son about the facts of life at all and that he is remiss in his role as father. The boy is now almost seventeen and six feet plus in height, and his mother is really worried. Yes, I believe it is the parental responsibility to assure adequate sex information, but if a father won't, then why can't a mother? Besides, I'd bet my boots that junior has already had quite an education—both factual and fictional. It is entirely possible and even probable that a father may not be able to handle these matters and still be a good father. So, Mom, get to work if you think your son needs it. And Dad, maybe you had better take another look at your relationship with that seventeen-year-old.

teenage pregnancy

sexual abuse of children

It is not easy to discuss the topic of pregnant girls in grades seven through twelve in the schools of our land. The situation is reaching epidemic proportions in large cities and in little places too. Our over-liberalized society has nearly sanctioned love on a contractual basis and marriage for the moment, and it will pay the price for it—indeed it is paying the price now. In the last six years some cities have experienced a 200 percent increase in teenage out-of-wedlock pregnancies. In one city there were 5,350 reported cases of venereal disease in youth, and this is less than one-tenth the real number. There are those who would blot out the problem by simply changing our view of marriage and the family. Until that unhappy day, we must face the miseries of countless children who are becoming mothers and fathers to only slightly younger children. A reawakening by all of us is urgently needed.

Even more prevalent and insidious than children being battered at home by their parents is the sexual abuse some children have to suffer at the hands of someone in the home. More than a million children twelve and over run away from home each year, and the statistics are shocking since they too often point to incest as the prime cause of the runaway act. Remember, we rarely ask the child to explain the reasons for his running. We usually assume that the runaway is wrong. He is then returned home only to face exactly what he ran away from. I have used *he* badly here, since incestuous relationships are most often between girls and their fathers or other males in the home. Over one-third of the girls in detention homes are there because they ran away time and again from fathers, uncles, cousins, boarders, and other males who sexually abused them. Too often these girls are put away for running away from a crime that is the fault of the adults in their world. It is the responsibility of judges and detention officers to carefully assess the reasons for a girl's running away.

teenage parents

learning homosexual behavior

There seems to be mounting evidence of the fact that teenage mothers and fathers do not provide adequately for their children. It is still true, despite the almost unbelievable adult statistics regarding divorce, that teenage marriage has the highest mortality rate of all marriages. It is not surprising, then, that those under eighteen make the worst parents. A ten-year follow-up on 172 children born to eighty-six under-eighteen mothers and eighty-six over-eighteen mothers shows that the children of younger mothers are developmentally inferior. They are more apt to be underweight and shorter and to have behavior difficulties, lower I.Q.s, and more reading problems. It is also true, however, that under-eighteen mothers are less anxious about their mothering than older mothers and are more likely to give their children opportunities for early independence. Despite this finding, their children were more dependent. I have frequently said that biological maturity is no sign of psychological maturity. It is tough enough to raise fine families when there is a reasonable degree of maturity. It is nearly impossible for a child to raise a child.

What leads young men into the "gay" life? It seems doubtful that many of them are suffering from a hormonal imbalance that would lead them into homosexuality. Most homosexual behavior is environmental. It is often in response to parents who voice disapproval of boys who are aesthetically motivated. Society too equates interest in art, literature, music, and dance with females. Obese boys, unathletic and overprotected, are frequently the butt of community sarcasm and rejection. Then where do they turn for approval? To those who approve of and appreciate their difference—and these are usually males or females who are similar in their likes. In my opinion, should our society agree more and more that there is no difference in homosexual and heterosexual behavior, should it continually accede to demands that sex-role identity be erased, then we may expect that more and more boys will choose homosexuality as their way of life. Males should strive to be emulated as males; likewise, girls need appropriate female sex-role models. Any great deviation from one's natural sex is unhealthy.

becoming homosexual

teenage bigotry

Apparently Freud hasn't answered the question of the cause of homosexuality in boys to the complete satisfaction of many. Freud said that homes where there are domineering mothers and passive or absent fathers are likely to produce sons who reject the male sex-role model. The hard evidence about this is not completely certain since not all homes with aggressive mothers and quiescent fathers produce homosexual sons. There is evidence that other factors can produce homosexuality. Homosexual patterns are not set only in preschool days. It is likely that the choice of rejecting the typical male role occurs because of negative experience with male siblings and with males in one's peer group. Often the move toward homosexuality progresses in slow steps heightened by homosexual experiences with older male relatives and friends. In adolescence the fear of not being able to behave adequately with girls (and this is not an uncommon fear) can progressively lead a normal boy to seek sexual satisfaction with other boys rather than to hassle with the conquest of females. And in our contemporary culture, nearly every medium now shows tolerance and approval of what has become an alternative life-style.

Just after World War II there was a great movement in the public schools to conscious decrease the virulent anti-Jewish feelings among high school youth in various parts of the country. A recent study of three integrated east coast public school districts has indicated a high incidence of anti-Jewish and anti-black prejudices. It appears that prejudice requires continual work if it is to be kept in check. The work in intergroup relations at the end of World War II was very effective, but it wasn't continued. Antisemitism among adolescents was linked to low family income and poor academic performance. The more deprived a youngster was, the more prejudiced against Jews he was. Black teenagers, although generally more deprived than whites, were less prejudiced against Jews as Jews. Blacks tended to be prejudiced against whites and did not make the distinction of whether the white was Jewish or Christian. Other findings of this study showed that non-Jewish teenagers, in overwhelming numbers, viewed Jewish teenagers as being intelligent, ambitious, and successful. There is bias among teenagers, and we need interfaith education badly.

affluent youth

the hospitalized adolescent

148 What's it like in a town where 27,000 people whose average incomes are well above the $15,000 mark live? In Westport, Connecticut, it is "like wild." It has been very reliably estimated that three-fourths of the town's youth have at one time or another experimented with some form of narcotics. One out of five youths has drug-related problems. There are as many as 250 addicts on heroin in this little affluent suburb. Eighty percent of the people under 25 who are in prison in Connecticut are there on drug or drug-related charges. One family related its sad tale of a son's progression from marijuana to heroin, and it is particularly interesting to discover that even after finding paraphernalia for heroin use around the house, even after he saw his own son spend hours in the bathroom, and despite seeing the hordes of kids who would occupy his son's room all night long, the father still would not let himself believe what was happening before his very eyes. The downward progression, which was filled with lies and deceit, and which eventually ended with a jail sentence, was a real shocker to this "hardened" reporter.

One of the really tough things about being an adolescent is that because you are eighteen or six-foot-five, adults expect you to act as though either height or the nearness to twenty-one were all that is necessary to insure adultlike behavior. The difficulties of the hospitalized adolescent are a good example of the dilemma adolescent youngsters are in whenever they are hospitalized for nonpsychiatric problems. The most important developmental task of adolescence is to gain a reasonable independence. At its best, hospitalization makes most patients uneasy and in many children causes regressions to former childish behaviors, such as tantrums and bed-wetting. Thus, adolescents are particularly hurt by hospitalization. They need help but are entirely dependent upon nurses, doctors, and staff opinions. There is little they can choose to do. It must be this way, generally speaking, but it hurts the developing psyche. In the adolescent ward of Boston Children's Hospital, patients and staff meet together and separately to discuss mutual problems. Hospitals don't need to dehumanize.

firstborn children

privacy

Much has been written and said about the differences between our firstborn children and those who follow. Ordinarily we become more secure parents as we have more children. There seems to be little doubt that we overinvest ourselves in our children who are born first. It is for this reason that they are often overachievers. It is also for this reason that we build up in firstborn children certain high expectancies that they are not always able to live up to. Dr. Jon Weiss in New York compared fourteen firstborn and later-born boys, all between the ages of twelve and fifteen. Each boy was placed in a series of stress-producing situations. They were then hooked up to machines that checked their heart rate when they were subjected to electric shocks, simple arithmetic problems, and mild criticism for their errors in arithmetic. There was a significant difference in the heart rate of the firstborns; that is, in most of the cases studied, firstborns had heart rates that were significantly faster than later-borns. Firstborns seem to develop more anxieties than later-borns, so their hearts react accordingly.

We all, children and adults, need to feel that the people we live with respect our privacy. It is urgent that when children lock or even close doors, their parents show the same respect that they expect when their doors are closed. But what if you suspect that things are going on behind those doors? The simple rule that needs to prevail here is that the child is more important than his privacy. The most frightening thing to an adolescent is the feeling that no one can control him. This means that every adolescent needs his parents' concern and control whenever they feel they need to intervene. The search for self in the adolescent years cannot be successful for the child if he thinks his parents don't really care. Of course, there is much rejection of parents by the adolescent. It must be that way because the youngster is trying on the world of separation, but he needs someone who cares what he does.

149

time-out

all honest work

150 All of us probably remember that wonderful expression of childhood, "Time-out!" It meant that whatever we were doing, whatever was happening that was going against us, we could use this magiclike incantation, and we would be free, untouched, able to breathe and recover. I am suggesting that time-out as a phrase used between children and parents is a valuable way to cool things off—at least for the moment, which is often all you will need to regain your sanity. Recently a mother of a thirteen-year-old called and said that she and her daughter had just had it out, both verbally and physically. They knew it and so did the whole neighborhood, which heard and witnessed it. I suggested to them that the time-out declaration be used as an emergency measure so that each of them or any one of them can, before real violence flares, stop the action. Can you see it? Just before you or your child is pushed over the brink of patience, someone calls for time-out, and that means everything going on stops. Wait ten minutes and start approaching the problem when you have cooled off.

Those who have children in college or nearly ready for an institution of higher learning might be interested in the outlook for admission into certain fields. For several years now we have had such an oversupply of elementary school teachers that many of my students at the University of Utah are taking jobs as teacher aides rather than not work. Columbia University Law School had 4,000 applications for 300 places. Yale Law expects 3,000 applications for 165 places. Medical school admissions are the same. Harvard reported that last year 300 of its seniors could not gain admission to any medical school. Nationally 60 percent of all applicants to medical school were turned down. It seems to me we must reorder priorities in our hearts as well as our schools. Not everyone should be a professional. Our nation needs intelligent plumbers, air-conditioning men, and building tradesmen. All honest work is worthwhile, and we as a nation must act as if we really believe it.

what's wrong with college

academic depression

William Shannon of the *New York Times* editorial board has written an article entitled "The New Barbarians," in which he deplores the retreat from responsibility in the colleges. Just what does he mean by this? He alludes to the fact that in many colleges, required courses are a thing of the past, teaching of the traditional curriculum in the arts and sciences has been abandoned, exams and formal grades are fast disappearing, students are designing their own courses, and the old-fashioned idea of a major field of study is nearly extinct. I have a few things to say about this. First, it is true that too many colleges are bowing to pressures that are tantamount to making college just a three- or four-year resting place. The odd instructor who insists upon work done finds himself rated G for goofy, and he becomes the department oddball. On the other hand, placing the responsibility for learning more upon the students is a first-rate trend for many but a dismal failure for most who have learned that the shortest route to a degree is the best. There is much to know, and you can't learn it in bull sessions.

Much is very wrong in the college and university world. There is now what is commonly called an academic depression. At the University of Utah Medical School, funds are available to admit only 100 of 1,400 applicants. The University of California at Berkeley is dropping 150 faculty jobs. In order to save $25,000 at the University of Kansas, the lawns were left uncut last summer. College graduates are no longer guaranteed jobs, and Ph.D.'s go begging. Students who were once activists have simmered down, and the only really live issues in most places are women's lib and homosexual freedom. If campuses are returning to a certain testy normality, the public isn't. Mr. Tax payer seems not to be able to forget student riots, long-haired agitators, and radical professors, and public as well as private institutions are paying the price. John Q. Public doesn't mind accepting the good life created largely by educated brains (TV, moon shots, frozen foods, high-powered rifles, plastic boats, and shiny autos), but he seems to reject the chance to pay for those educated minds that went to work inventing them.

151

college admissions

what keeps them out of college

152 Traditionally, high schools blame their excellent but rigid academic requirements on the demands for admission to universities. So in New York City, David Abramson studied the entrance requirements of 100 colleges throughout the country and discovered that there is much myth behind the idea that high school courses of study have to be concentrated in the five big academic areas. Historically the high schools have been requiring sixteen to twenty units divided between these five areas. Actually, this study reports, the colleges require ten units divided between the five subjects, with heavy emphasis on English and social studies. The high school is in a unique position to make a real difference in the intellectual and social life of young people and has too long been a miniature college, priding itself on its hideboundness. We at the college level are traditional enough. Let the high schools be intellectually independent and teach what kids really need to know. "Develop the youngster in high school as your community sees its needs, and worry less about college admissions," is Abramson's advice.

It is not always just brains that count when it comes to entrance to college. A survey of 10,000 high school students showed that it was primarily the lack of encouragement from parents that kept out many children whose parents were blue-collar and unskilled workers. These people, known as lower-class working parents, too often have an indifferent attitude toward education beyond high school, and no matter how bright their children are, there just isn't the parental push that seems to make the difference. All of this is particularly sad since many of the lower class youngsters have the ability and talent to do well in college. On the other hand, contrast this figure to that of the sons of professional parents—over 75 percent of these youngsters enter college regardless of their ability. While it might be nice to think about, the myth of the parent who didn't have much education yet dreams the American dream of a better life for his child just isn't the case. Too many lower-class parents don't push their children into the college arena. Brains and anxious parents make the difference.

a quiet revolution   crime on campus

There are plenty of noisy revolutions in the world, but one of the quiet revolutions now going on concerns college graduates who simply will not take advanced degrees and who instead turn to taxi driving or other nonintellectual jobs. I have nothing against taxi drivers—indeed, some of the best families I know have been well supported by fathers who drove cabs—but I am concerned that the reservoir of brain power that is trained will dwindle. Four years ago ninety Harvard seniors were undecided about their careers. A survey last month indicated that over 250 were undecided. In 1966, 27 percent said they aspired to the PH.D. degree; last year that figure was down to 14 percent. To some this may be just great, since too many Ph.D.'s are overeducated. But let's face it: the great technology we now enjoy came largely from highly trained men. Intellect isn't everything, but it helps.

The picture of the peaceful, shady, tree-lined campus that I attended years ago is a thing of the past. *The National Observer* surveyed campuses from coast to coast and found that rape, robbery, and assault are virtually every-day happenings. On the Pennsylvania State University campus, for instance, ROTC students now patrol the walk from the library to the dorms. The only police-man on our campus in 1943 was a retired older man who was known to everyone and who never did more than pick up a piece of paper occasionally. Crime on a campus? We never heard of it! At the University of Utah, for a long time a very safe place to go to school, our police force is now young, vigorous, fully trained, unarmed, and respected. Our police have full arrest powers, and when you are in violation, you report not to the campus but to city magis-trates. At New Mexico State University crime has jumped 19 percent in one year, and this is due to the growth of a police department that now sees and apprehends more. At the risk of seeming to be one who yearns only for the past, I must admit that things just ain't what they used to be.

university sex code

154 When the University of Michigan's student-dominated housing board dropped from its housing code a rule that explicitly barred cohabitation, overnight visitation, and premarital sexual intercourse, there were some very excited parents and alumni around the countryside. I know of no way, short of a policeman in every car or dormitory room, to prohibit sexual behavior, but I am certain that no university ought to make it any easier. Although I have, from time to time, twitted women's liberation for what I consider to be good reason, I am on their side when they preach that women are not mere vessels, simply objects to be conquered. That they are is a barbarian viewpoint not at all unknown in decadent societies. Double standards are never easy to live with, but every girl has a father, and you will recall the old expression that said, "Remember, she may be somebody's daughter." It is not prudery or Victorianism for a university to specifically prevent and admonish students in their sexual behavior within its own dormitories.

parents (of all ages!)

In 1965 George H. Frank, in his article "The Role of the Family in the Development of Psychopathology" *(Psychological Bulletin* 65 (1965), pp. 191-205), summarized research on the influence of the family on human development and concluded that nothing had been discovered about the effect of child-rearing practices on the personalities of children. Interestingly enough, in his psychology text entitled *Children* (Holt, Rinehart & Winston, 1967), Boyd McCandless said this: "On the basis of our actual contact as parents, teachers and professional workers, we 'know in our hearts' that Frank is wrong."

In other words, though there is scanty research evidence that the influence of parents on children's growth and development, physically, socially, and emotionally, is a very important factor, there is nonetheless what I should like to call "gut" or "hard" evidence that there is no such thing as the parents' having no influence upon the children. In fact, quite the opposite is so. The influence that parents have on children is quite obviously enduring and pervasive. In Robert Freedman's book *Family Roots of School Learning and Behavior Disorders* (Charles E. Thomas Co., 1973) and in numerous other volumes,

we have continual allusions to the influence of parents upon the developing child.

While it's true that there is very likely a sixty-forty ratio of genetics to environment in the personality makeup of children, it is also true that at this moment in scientific time, it is impossible to do anything in the way of altering the genetic makeup of the child. So even though genetics may account for better than half of what a child eventually becomes, it is to no avail since there are no means available to juggle the genes. We are left with the remaining 40 percent known as environmental influence.

The most significant part of that environment is the first five to six years that a child spends with his parents. In a study of 200 college students who were successful in college,* it was found that every single one of them traced their successful adjustment to adolescence and their college careers to their parents and family. Further testimony may be found in the work of Christopher Jencks in his volume entitled *Equality of Education*. Here he documents voluminously the fact that it doesn't make any differ-

---

*James A. Knight, "Resisting the Call of the Cave," *Medical Insight*, 1970, vol. 2, pp. 67-77.

adults are models of love

ence what you teach in school or who teaches the children. The only thing that counts in success in school is the economic status of the parents. I would be willing to go so far as to say that not only is the economic status of the parents a major determining factor in school success, but the overall mental health of the parents and their concepts of discipline and interpersonal relationships with their children are the major factors in whether or not the children will grow up to be able to cope with life's problems. It is interesting to report that the following six or seven features were described by these students as being the particular behaviors of their parents that were especially influential in their college success: (1) firmness, (2) direction, (3) rules that make sense, (4) high expectations of all family members, (5) mutual trust and respect, and (6) the knowledge that they were somebody.

It is still probably accurate to say that as the twig is bent, so grows the tree. It would be the height of folly for parents to ever conclude or behave as if they were an inconsequential part of the experience of childhood.

Parents frequently complain that everyone talks about love to them but few actually show mothers how to be loving and how to instill love in their children. The best model for a child is to see a father or mother in love with a spouse. The first requirement for learning love is living with it. Children need to see how people in love behave toward one another. I think an example from my own life may serve the purpose well, but it may not make it easier for me to return home this evening. My wife and I, both fairly volatile people, often disagree about things. Things even get quite heated, and the kids on occasion think that we must be very unhappy. But long ago we resolved never to let these momentary things affect us for too long so it isn't too long before we are back to normal again. Children need to know that life is full of ups and downs but that love reunites, heals, and often makes life lovely. After all, half the fun of argument is making up, isn't it? Thus, adults provide models of love and children learn to count the ways long before they know the poem.

the parental function

parents provide models

Back in the nineteenth century, Joseph Smith, the first prophet-president of The Church of Jesus Christ of Latter-day Saints, was asked how he managed to govern his far-flung, heterogeneous band of disciples. He answered in a brilliant way: "I teach them correct principles, and they govern themselves." It has occurred to me that herein lies the answer to the question of building self-discipline in children. Let me warn those who foolishly think that children will govern themselves without any principles that part of the parental function is the inculcation of ideals that eventually need to become internalized. At certain times in the life of the child, certain principles his parents have may indeed be questioned, even discarded. All that this world requires of parents is that they teach the correct principles, and then the responsibility for behavior is increasingly placed upon the heads of the children. The sounds of freedom echo with a hollowness when everything goes. By the same principle, ideals that stifle or prevent the development of freedom strangle the spirit of childhood.

There are many adults who provide only super avant-garde models for their children to follow, rather than help those children learn to come to grips with their own individuality. Parents who are "just because" people are those who will do everything and anything the last advertisement said was in. They cannot expect anything from their children but what has been termed other-directed behavior. That is, their children's manners, dress, outlets for recreation, and so forth will always be what the other fellow does or has. We want to try to grow inner-directed children, or those who do their own thing because something inside them tells them it is good rather than because everybody is doing it. In an age when we hear the phrase "doing one's own thing" bandied about quite a bit, I have great difficulty in finding parents and others doing what they really want to do. Instead, they tend to be carbon copies of whatever the last fashion ad tells them to wear. Be original; forget what "they" say is in.

the foundation of children's values

parents' values

What values are relevant for children to cherish in tomorrow's world? This is the question raised by Bill Shannon of the *New York Times*. He recently told parents that if a child is to learn to be an adult, he has to begin by respecting the adults he knows. Respect is love's complement. By learning to obey his father and mother, a child has freedom, within the sure boundaries they set, to discover his own identity. These personal questions will tell you if you have raised a maverick or a human. Does he tell the truth to others and to himself? Does he work or shirk? Can he articulate and channel aggression? Can he show tenderness and compassion to other people? Can he be trusted with a job, with money, with responsibility for another person's welfare? Is he using his talents? Love and discipline are the foundation of values. If parents do not exert their values, the media will, and there is evidence that our children are being raised with Madison Avenue's values. The abdication of the parent to outside-the-family influences is a serious threat to raising fine families.

American children are suffering from widespread parent failure. So said William Shannon, member of the editorial board of the *New York Times* and the father of three boys aged nine, four, and two months, in a blistering article in the *New York Times*. He goes on to say that mothers and fathers are paralyzed by uncertainty because they really don't know what their values are, and if they do understand them, they doubt they have the right to structure their own child's attitudes, beliefs, and conduct. We know much about the developing child. We know, for example, that his first twelve years are crucial to his later conduct. What is lacking is not information but conviction. Mr. Shannon goes on to acidly attack parents who are afraid of their own values. Inevitably, he says, there is a gap between each generation in a family, and there should be. It does not matter, he adds, whether boys wear hair shoulder length or crew cut, collect Sinatra or Dylan records. What does matter is how they treat other people and how people treat them.

three types of parents

parental standards

Most parents can be described as either permissive, authoritative, or authoritarian. Let me define each. The authoritarian parent is one who believes that either the father or mother is omnipotent, omniscient, and reigns supreme. In the permissive home the parents feel that just so long as there are love and human relations skills, all will be well. The authoritative parent is right in the middle. He knows that children need limits and boundary lines. The evidence today is that the home without structure and control produces youngsters who are moral casualties. Peer pressures are very strong in the direction of deviance from accepted moral standards. In order for a child to withstand these pressures or to minimize them, he needs to have a code that is clear and firm. The business of right and wrong being relative is hardly applicable in the case of young children who are not able to make these subtle differentiations. Don't be afraid to take a stand and stay with it. The kids may yell, but they'll respect you.

One of the arguments the counterculture tries to foist upon the straight population is that a man has the right to do whatever he pleases with his own body. This is a gross oversimplification of man's place in the world. Children must not be allowed to grow up thinking that it is nobody's business but their own whether they take into their bodies harmful substances. Each child is the child of another person, and each man usually becomes the parent of another child. To react to the threats of this terribly complicated society by retreating into inner space and to total self-centeredness is the beginning of the destruction of the race. Children need to be taught to be other-centered, to realize that in no way do they act alone. To become all that is possible, man must remember that he is social and that he must live in groups. It is high time for parents to withdraw from a glorification of youth, decide where they stand, and enforce these standards with their children. Every adult parent must formulate values and live by and with them. Anything less creates sociopathic children.

the whys of parent behavior

adolescent adults

162 Americans worship experience. Parents in trouble with their children nearly always feel better when they find out from others what they do with their children. People like radio programs that outline specific procedures for doing the right thing with children. It's what works that counts. A familiar commercial once had as its main line, "It's what's up front that counts." I take this to mean, when translated into noncommercial language, that what we think is very important. At all professional conferences today it is not the least uncommon to have someone explain the thinking behind the doing. Theoretically (and I know we shy away from theory as if it wasn't worthy of real attention, especially as our three-year-old is nagging the life out of us), every parent should be able to give a good reason for every at-home action he takes. Thus, if you strike the child, you should have thought it out first. If you decide to say no, you should be able to give some reasonable explanation for your decision. Why you are doing what you are doing is very important.

Allow me to quote Dr. Bill Schul in the magazine *Christian Home*. He wrote: "Millions of American parents are today rearing little, old children—little in that fathers and mothers delay far longer than parents of other lands the introduction of the child to the responsibilities of useful living, and old in the sense that our youngsters are hurled into sophisticated living at a far more tender age than most of the world's children. It is not surprising that the spoiled teenager is refusing to grow up. He can receive the privileges of adulthood without the responsibilities. And when his parents talk about the good old days of their youth, along with foolish attempts at aping today's young people, the teenager is not so sure he wants anything to do with the grown-up world." Adolescent adults have never been very good models for the young. Youth searches for people who know where they are and are not drifters with each new passing philosophy or fad.

the child within

starting a parent group

There is a baby lying in wait within each of us. By this, I mean that childish behavior is part of every human being's repertoire of responses to the human situation. It sounds a bit complicated, so allow me to develop an example. When a child does not get what he wants, he often pouts, becomes aggressive, or goes into a temper tantrum. As we mature, we tend to diminish these kinds of immature reactions in our routine behavior. To the extent that anger, vituperation, and hostility are relegated to those rare occasions when we blow our cool, we may be said to be becoming more mature. Yet just below the surface of each adult lies the waiting baby with its immature reactions fo the stresses of life. Children react easily to frustration with childish behavior. So, too, do adults revert to this behavior when reasonableness has been tested to the limit. Our immature behavior is the child within us.

Once W. C. Fields told parents to fly away and let their children (he called them "the little rotters") fend for themselves. Well, lots of parents aren't afraid to face the problems of raising children, so they have formed a group in Virginia called "The Parent Place." It's a place to talk, listen, and swap notes on successes and agonies in rearing children. This seems to me to be a wise use of parent power, and I would advocate that others do the same. We spend millions a year learning to bowl, improve our golf game, and shoot pictures with zoom lenses, but not one cent is spent on learning how to rear children more effectively. There is much knowledge in a group meeting to discuss common problems. Even more important is the fact that people, especially those who live somewhere near one another, are getting together to attack problems in common. Furthermore, if they share certain ideals and values that develop from these talks, their children will face a more or less common set of values shared by their parents. When they find many parents agreeing upon principles, the kids will even be mystified. No need to leave the rotters alone. Don't fail parenthood. Get together in a parent group.

worry clinics

learning to be parents

164 The use of "worry clinics" for parents seems to me to be a useful way of helping parents share their problems. The four most worrisome areas of child and family growth are the youth rebellion, anger, the new morality, and father's influence, in that order. Parents are most worried about whether or not their kids will survive hippiedom communes, running away, and defiance against all forms of authority. Somewhat surprising is the number two item—anger. Parents are very concerned about their inability to keep their tempers and are also disturbed about their children's displays of anger. Almost all parents are concerned about the free attitude toward sexual behavior and the apparent lack of concern their children have for conventional morality. Finally, harried mothers are concerned that their husbands, even in this day of liberation, are evading their share of child-rearing responsiblities. The only hope is the fact that they are not alone in their worries. Group discussions lower our sense of isolation and get us out of the house.

The horrible statistics regarding divorce, desertion, and childbeating in the U.S. should prompt educators throughout the nation to reassess just what is important in the education of our children. I am now quite ready to forcefully advocate child development and family development courses from the fifth grade through the high school years. While having good parents is the best education for one's own parenthood, there isn't enough of it to pass around. So it seems that if drivers' education is a valid course of study, and I believe it is, then surely it is not impossible to take the next step and realize that rearing human beings is at least as important as carburetors and stop signs. Twisted, hurt, and incorrigible families do not, however, end up on slabs in morgues where bodies can be counted as they are in auto crashes. Need we wait for this type of evidence?

rearing responsible children

super - mod parents

Some down-to-earth advice on discipline at home comes from Dr. James Dobson's book *Dare to Discipline*. He makes five key points about helping children behave within reasonable limits. First, he says that developing respect for parents is essential to all later relationships. The child who knows he can do as he pleases at six will do what he pleases at sixteen. Second, he maintains that if you punish a child, the best time to maintain real communication is immediately after punishment when you show how much you really love him despite the fact that you were pretty upset earlier. Third, control without nagging is essential. No child likes to be badgered. Set time limits, stay with them as best you can, and you won't have to nag. Next, don't saturate a child with excessive materialism. Getting everything you can afford may be worse than deprivation. Fifth, neither excessive love nor rejection is good for developing discipline. Responsible children come from responsible, reasonably controlling parents.

One of the odd things about American culture today is the apparent willingness of forty-year-olds to behave like, dress like, and speak the language of young people in the drug culture. Now before you start to label me a ridiculous right winger, stop and remember that when children start to experiment with drugs, with language, and with dress styles that their parents deplore, they frequently see this attempt to be with it as part of their parents' behavior. I was surprised at an esteemed professional meeting in Washington, D. C., to note that even the language of the mature was so hip and culture-conscious that it almost seemed as if the adult world was attempting to beat the young adolescents at their own game. Children need parents who know how to resist fads and ideals that are transient. In raising early adolescents, we must always be thinking in terms of further developing the child's ability to cope with human relations problems. Super-mod dress and manners aren't especially becoming to those who are over thirty.

buddy - buddy parents

love their mother

166 You may be old enough to remember the song that went, "I don't want a buddy, I just need a sweetheart," or some such words, and if you do, you might appreciate the relevance or those lyrics to the parent-child relationship. A buddy relationship with a child is apt to be carried too far so that the buddy parent does not provide the model of guidance and discipline that a child needs. He needs that model far more than he needs an exaggerated oneness. Dads who dress like their kids and hang out with their kids (just like all the other kids) are overdoing the role of buddy. A child needs to feel that his parents feel for him and with him more than that they are exactly like him. To be deprived of a reasonable adult image is a sad experience in childhood. Children, like adults, need to have goals—things to aspire to, people to live up to—and their buddy-buddy parents often provide only companionship. Too often parents go overboard to hide their own guilt feelings, and this doesn't give the child what he needs.

It has been said that the most important thing a father can do for his children is to love their mother. The wisdom of the statement is obvious. When children see love about them, when there is love at home, they can model their own behavior after what they see and hear. Love is caught, not taught. Despite the many statistics about overpopulation that are rather grim, I like to recall what one Nobel Prize winner once said when quizzed about overpopulation. He said that the world has always been in need of not fewer people, but of better, more loving ones. A good marriage is often the result of a loving childhood. I have frequently put it this way: A girl who has been well-loved by her father will more easily be loved by a husband. Why? Because she has learned to return love offered to her mother and herself.

mothering styles · helping mothers at home

While it is undoubtedly true that children have their own growth and personality styles, it is equally true that mothers their own mothering styles. In other words, each child and each mother has his own temperament, and these can be observed clashing or meshing at various times. It is just as possible to have a clash of personality between mother and child as it is between child and teacher. Some mothers, for instance, enjoy the early years of childhood, mostly because they enjoy the utter dependency of the child. Then when the preschool years roll around, what was once a placid relationship can break out into a violent dislike, not because mother is a mean or horrible ogre, but because her mothering style has been offended. I've seen mothers who didn't like the dependency relationship characterized by the early years, but they were tops as mothers of adolescents because their mothering style doted upon the interchange of adultlike observations mingled with the erraticisms of adolescence. So, mothers, whatever troubles you may be having with one of your brood now may not be the result of a defect of yours but is more possibly a clash of living styles between your child and yourself.

Since the 1950s it has been axiomatic that bad homes are better for children than good institutions. Now you might think that you have read wrong, but the truth of the matter is, even though parents may not be very educated, even though they may even be quite careless, there is a bond between parents, even bad parents, and their children that never develops between excellent teachers and those they teach. Since there is doubt that Head Start and other federal programs have a long-lasting effect on the growth and development of children, there is much interest in helping mothers to educate their children at home under the kind but watchful eye of a trained professional. What mother wants to be told that she isn't up to the task of good child rearing? None. So bear in mind that nearly all mothers want the same three things for their children as they grow up: good performance in school, a good job, and a fulfilling life. Experts enter homes and ask only what they can do for the betterment of the child. And it works.

children of working mothers

boys and moms

A problem that we are facing nearly everywhere today, a problem that will not just go away, is the employment of mothers outside the home. A study of 466 children of working mothers and 466 children of stay-home mothers showed that the children of working mothers were more aggressive, more demanding, more emotionally immature, more insecure, and less academically motivated, and they identified less well with the parent of the same sex. This doesn't have to happen, but it does. In order to prevent such problems, it is important that mothers never leave the impression that they are working for the child or because the father can't provide. It is also unproductive for the mother to remind the child of how tired she is, and to substitute material things for human love and affection.

For many years we have flayed motherhood as the chief perpetrator of bad feelings in the home. Philip Wylie in his book *Generation of Vipers* called the disease "momism." Modern writers have laid the unrest and rebellion of youth at the doorstep of motherhood. Many years ago Freud talked about the resolution of conflict that must occur between a boy and his father through age six or thereabouts. It seems that this conflict or rivalry for mastery of wife and mother doesn't necessarily end at a tender age. Much thought has been given to the notion that it often has residual effects during adolescence. Consider the probability that young men in their early teens still feel some of the hatred, fear, and love they felt earlier. I was playing Ping-Pong with my thirteen-year-old son the other night, and the intensity of his assault, the almost franticness of his desire to beat me seemed very evident. Incidentally, his over-forty father keenly felt this rivalry but also had to feel that he hadn't lost all of his skill, so I really bent to the task of wiping him out. I did it, but not with the ease of years gone by.

who gets the child?

father's role

The very knotty and emotion-laden problem of nearly always assigning the custody of children to their mothers is an important one to discuss in today's world. I see every justification for giving a mother her children when the children are in the first year or two of life. Note that I used the term *her* children as if the youngsters didn't belong to the father at all. I think this is a bias that has been built into many of us. After children are a few years old, I think that there may be numerous times when, because of the particulars of a situation, a father may justly be given legal custody. Many times mothers have to go out to work, and thus the children are left with some baby-sitter or child-care service. There appears little reason that fathers would not be as able to contract for these services as mothers are. Most fathers don't seem to show the courts an interest in their young children, and so nine out of ten preschoolers are given to their mothers. Interesting possiblities here, aren't there?

The importance of a good father in the growing-up process was recently emphasized when poor fathering was found to be linked with an increase of suicides in adolescent girls. Paternal deprivation is the term used for deficient father-child relationships. Army psychiatrists have traced the overmasculinization of certain males to poor father relationships. Young soldiers feel forced to adopt exaggerated masculinity to cover up their fear of femininization. In other words, when weak or ineffectual fathers are part of the growing-up process, a young man may begin to dream about feminine things because of the dominance of feminine things in his life, and so he overplays his masculinity to assure himself that he is a man. I would say that an emotionally immature father is one who has temper tantrums, who purposely doesn't come home, who resorts to excessive physical exercise or excessive drinking, and who is so completely dominated by his wife that it is clear to everyone in the family. All or some of these are signs of immaturity.

169

fathers and sons   boys and parental consistency

170 One of the really startling discoveries I have run across in the past few years says that the average amount of time fathers spend with fifth-grade sons is seven and a fourth minutes per week. Research evidence tells us that a boy's relationship with his father is the most important factor in his growth of conscience, his creativity, his ability to learn, and his concept of himself as a male. I would urge every father to rather quietly check his clock this week and figure how much time he spends not only with his sons but with all his children. If your figure looks as bad as the one I just quoted, don't blame anyone but yourself when your son tells you one day to bag it when you make a harmless inquiry. If you conscientiously chart this time spent, you will automatically start to increase it. What is more important than setting a model for another human? If you leave it to the schools or the Scoutmaster, it may not get done. Look to it; you are now informed.

Parental consistency has been identified as one of the major factors in the elementary school performance of boys. When parents are consistent in their guidance, boys come to see that their rewards and punishments are directly related to their behavior and are the consequences of their acts. Consistency means that children, through their parents' actions, come to know what to expect when they behave or misbehave. Inconsistency means that the child may be rewarded for an act one time and punished for the same act another time. When the home is a source of steady behavior, children find the motivation necessary to excellent performance in school. I was interested to learn from the work of Dr. Gunars Reimanis of Corning Community College that these findings applied only at the elementary school level and only to boys. A further report of his study indicates that it is very possible to turn around the bad behavior of boys in school through the intensive effort of teachers and counselors. Boys, it seems, flower under the warm light of affirmation and encouragement.

fathers and infants

talking with dad

Dr. Robert Pickett of Syracuse University reports in a *PTA Magazine* article that white, upper-middle-class fathers were clocked in a study as having spent an average of twenty-six seconds per day with their infant children. I needn't here reiterate my dismay at some of the more violent women's liberation movement stances, but I must confess that they are on very firm ground when they maintain that child rearing is not the exclusive domain of women. Those fathers who see their task as over at conception are in for a rude shock when they discover that the children they fathered don't really know who their fathers are. Except for breast-fed babies, there is no reason whatever for fathers not sharing in the nightly escapades of hungry, crying babies. Dads, share not only biology, but your arms and hearts, too.

The proper role for a father is becoming increasingly more difficult to define. Walking with my twelve-year-old on a recent Sunday, however, indicated to me that all is not lost. As we left the front door Stewart said, "Well, what shall we talk about?" It has been our custom, whenever taking some protracted time together, to select a topic for discussion, Our topic this week was the effects of emotions upon physical health. No role for father? Not by a long shot! Years ago, father was the judge; the role he played was to pass on the accumulated wisdom of the race. He was religious tutor. There are those who now see this role as outdated. I don't agree. Children need to know what their parents believe, where they have lived, and what they have lived for—the scope of father's world. I don't necessarily see father as the final arbiter, but as one who shares his decision-making powers with his wife. There will always be room for a show of love and affection, always room for talking about Dad's adolescent turmoils.

playing with children

dads, again

172 Fathers are important play companions for children. The trouble is that too many of them wait until their kids are old enough to play ball. Naturally four- and five-year-old sons are no match for their fathers, so dad tosses the ball a few times. Junior, or course, can't catch it or throw it back, and dad finally quits in disgust. The idea is to meet the child in play at his level with trucks, blocks, and other childlike toys so that father and son are participating on the same level. In this instance dad is not big and junior little. They are nearly equals because both are playing at something where each can be successful. If fathers only indulge in games that require physical skills, then sons are bound to be failures. After a few failure experiences, neither wants to play with the other, and what could have developed into a great friendship collapses into a relationship tinged with disgust. But when the two are playing with trucks, there is a magnificent equality that builds a fun, creative relationship.

Parents are in every sense the architects of their family's experience, and it is important that they plan the at-home experiences for their children much as the architect does the building he is drawing. Fathers are an integral part of this unit. Most dads, as well-meaning as they are, think that they are only the breadwinners and that the lives of the children are the affair of mother. While it is still true that mothers are the prime sources of affection and guidance, it is urgent that fathers consider that they are important models for both their sons and their daughters. A son must learn to behave like a man, to assume the generally conceded male roles; a daughter must learn to become a woman. Girls who learn to dislike their fathers find it difficult to assume the role of wife. Similarly, boys who hate their fathers don't make the best husbands. Fathers need to consciously decide to have more to do with their children and not leave it to chance and to mother.

self-control of adults

moms and dads

The story is told of a man who was pushing a grocery cart containing a screaming infant around a crowded supermarket. The man kept repeating softly, "Now there, Alan, don't get excited. Keep calm, Alan." A lady standing nearby, no doubt a mother herself, sought to console the desperate father and said, "You certainly should be commended for trying to sooth baby Alan." The man looked at her and said, with a solemn, straight face, "Lady, I'm Alan." A serious side of this story has to do with parents and teachers who sometimes panic as their children act out rage or discomfort. A certain way to guarantee that the screaming behavior will repeat itself is to develop a panic reaction. So our distraught father, who tried to calm himself by talking to himself, was, in fact, doing just the right thing. A little self-control goes a long way when children are letting off steam.

I have previously stated that it is my belief that there is a strong biological difference between men and women, and that difference accounts for the degree of nurturing afforded children by their mothers. Radical feminists will see in this some grand design for excluding father from his responsibility. Not so at all! I am convinced that most men do not comprehend the degree of affection and nurturing they can exhibit. Women are more biologically suited to their role as mothers, and I doubt that any type of legislation will change that. This does not say that some men may not have stronger feelings for children than do women. It does say that other things being equal, women are geared for the development of strong affectional ties with their offspring. A study indicates that it is the presence in the home of the father that is the major factor in the academic success of his children. Boys in four different categories were studied: boys without fathers all of their lives, boys whose dads were home only a few hours per week, boys who had not had fathers since they were five, and boys whose fathers were home several hours a day. Those who saw their fathers every day did best in school.

valuing parental opinion

viewers, not doers

174 We tend to believe that as life progresses for our children, our influence as parents diminishes. A survey of over 1,000 adolescents indicated that the contrary is true. Indeed, if children have over the years accepted their parents' right to influence them, then when they become adolescents and subject to the ideas of much wider community, they will still see their parents' ideas as useful. I was interested to learn that neither punishment nor reward is a significant factor in parents' ability to influence their teenagers; both of these depend upon parental observation of children's behavior; and in this age of automobiles, the mobility of children takes them beyond the range of parental surveillance. If children have been taught to consult with their parents, they will continue to do so until they have their own families. Valuing what parents say during adolescence may be nearly invisible, but it is patently clear that adolescents are keen to hear advice. Cheer up, then; all is not lost, even in this world of chaos.

Cliché or not, much evidence has been accumulated to show that the family that does things together nurtures children who will be doers when they get out on their own. The amount of action in a family—group or family biking, golf, tennis, skiing, hiking, or whatever—determines to a great extent the action pattern the children will follow for the rest of their lives. If parents do nothing in active sports, if all they do is view together, the children will grow up to be viewers, not doers. Action sports for the entire family need to be built into the family early, or else parents guarantee that their children will be sitters. Recent research indicates that sedentary parents produce sedentary children. When the family participates in sports together, parents and children are kept close, and the shared enjoyment of their sports activities provides communication avenues. Playing together today usually produces children who will be healthier and happier tomorrow.

diagnosing your family

self-worth in a family

An at-home diagnosis of your family's state of emotional health is not impossible, though I can guarantee that it will be somewhat uncomfortable. A family is a social system in and of itself, comprised of a number of individuals who have joined together to perpetuate the race. The two adults who start the family ought to be fully functioning human beings. Ideally they possess these characteristics: They are people who are honest and real and willing to take risks. They are creative. They feel competent and willing to look at themselves and the world and to recreate either should they find certain dissatisfactions. They are physically alive, mentally alert, and spiritually healthy. Both husband and wife need to be healthy humans in order to provide the kind of family soil that will grow similarly endowed children who will become healthy both physically and emotionally.

In order for a family to function happily, its members need to feel a reasonable degree of self-worth. Parents who form this coalition designed to develop humans who will be able to cope with the world and themselves need to feel more good about themselves than bad. I know these two words are scare words and at opposite ends of the mental health spectrum; nevertheless, in any family where there is evidence in either of the parents of deep feelings of disgust for self, there is greater probability of family failure. It is perfectly normal to be despondent at times. Who isn't numb at the end of a day of trying to steer a family ship that has three preschoolers at home and bundles of diapers and ironing always lurking around the corner? But though none of us can always feel great about ourselves, we should be able to say that most of time we are satisfied with our looks, our whys, and our wherefores. If this is not so, then one of the prime ingredients of the healthy family is lacking. A positive program of building these feelings needs to be looked at and something done about it.

developing listening skills

family rules

Everyone talks about family communication as if it means talking. However, for parents and spouses it means listening above all. Listening, you see, is learning behavior. As we grow, we learn our listening habits. Have you known people who listen on the run? Have you known others who simply don't listen? Listening is a reciprocal act, which means that if someone is speaking, someone ought to listen. This requires stopping long enough to be able to repeat what was said. Many of us listen rather carelessly; our ears hear, but our minds do not register. If the children in your family or your spouse says you don't really listen, you may be certain that they are correct. Even if they're not, their perceptions are valid. To listen, one needs to stop, meet the other person's eyes, get down to his level if necessary, and be able to make some response right then and there.

An important ingredient in a healthy family is the type of rules that govern that family. There are two kinds of rules. The first are overt or explicit ones—those rules that everyone agrees on and understands. The second are covert or implicit rules, those rules that suddenly arise and are usually manufactured by parents. These are rules that a child cannot abide by, since he never knew they were rules. Yet every family needs rules as much as a nation needs laws. Will you try this? Sit down with your family tonight and try to find out what they think the family rules are. If it turns out that they know of none, then you've got repair work to do. Draw up a reasonable set of rules with the children involved. Rules help straighten out troubled families.

families and porcupines

what he means counts

I have spent years talking about nearly every kind of family problem imaginable. Sometimes I wonder how there can be so many problems to talk about year in and year out. One thing seems to be clear: the proposition that good families produce good children. If children do have problems, they come from a problem family. And what family isn't a problem family? I know of no couple who are entirely without problems. Would it help any if I said that each parent needs to realize that in any marriage there are two people who decide to live and share together and who come from two different sets of parents? Thus their backgrounds are entirely different. As a couple merge into a new unit, they must, like the porcupines who were freezing and decided to get close to one another, find exactly the right distance between them so that they keep warm yet don't prick one another. Each couple must accommodate for the background, ideals, and habits with which the other came to the new union. They must decide which strange behaviors can be set aside as being inconsequential to the marriage.

It isn't unusual for rejecting mothers to report that their child keeps asking them if they love him. The usual story is that the mother says, "I tell him over and over that I love him, and yet he still asks me if I do." It isn't too unusual for children at one time or another to ask if their parents love them; it is usual for a child to persist in this query. If he does, then it is a sure sign of some anxiety about the matter, and usually that concern is based on some type of rejection behavior by the adults in his life that is not perceived by them. It is important for parents to try to develop a sensitivity to what the child *means* by what he says, rather than to attend to only what he *says*. For instance, when my daughter asks me somewhat plaintively about wearing some piece of inappropriate clothing to a dance, I know when to say no, and when I do, she breathes a sigh of relief. All along, you see, she is sending me the message of fear and doubt by her body, voice, and attitude. Listen with your third ear. It hears plenty.

building the self   calling children names

A major task of the early growth and development of children is the maturation of a positive self-image. Parents who start to have troubles whth their children at any age often do so because they love the children too much and don't enjoy them enough. Too many mothers who themselves are in need of love and who too often feel that they are unloveable learn to lavish love on their children when, in fact, what the child needs is understanding and a chance to develop. Love-hungry mothers often get their love from their children instead of their husbands, and thus they view the thrusts of the child toward independence as rejections of themselves. A child must continually exhibit antidependent behavior in order to grow up independent enough to make it on his own. Love for a child cannot be based on parental self-doubt, because this doesn't consider the welfare of the child. The young child who is loved too much never has a chance to develop an authentic self-image, because he is expected to behave in certain ways to please his parents. Through giving too much, the parent can actively undermine the child's self-confidence.

It has been said that labels are libelous. Thus when we call children *stupid, slob, liar,* and other epithets that reflect adult feelings, we are attacking the self-esteem of the child. Labeling words cover a multitude of things about a child, many of which are not true about the specific behavior to which we object, For instance, if a child has not made his bed one morning and we call him lazy, we are not describing the true situation. While this might accurately describe the present state of his room in relation to bedmaking, it also tends to say that he is lazy about everything else he does. This may not be the case. In fact, it may be that he isn't the least bit lazy about many other things. A child can take a specific comment about his room, such as, "You really left your bed in a mess." What he suffers from is the word *lazy.* We need to criticize by avoiding name calling and referring specifically to the act we wish the child to improve upon.

memo from your child

parents not all to blame

In a "Memorandum from Your Child," which contains twenty-two of the wisest advice items on how to bring up a better child, I have chosen some suggestions for parents that seem to be outstanding in their sagacity: Don't use force with me. It teaches me that power is all that counts, and I will respond more readily to being led. Don't be inconsistent. That confuses me and makes me try harder to get away with everything I can. Don't ever think that it is beneath your dignity to apologize to me. An honest apology makes me feel surprisingly warm toward you. Don't make me feel smaller than I am. I will make up for it by behaving like a big shot. Don't protect me from consequences. I need to learn from experience. Don't ever suggest that you are perfect or infallible. It gives me too much to live up to. Don't put me off when I ask honest questions. If you do, you will find that I will stop asking and will seek my information elsewhere. Don't let my fears arouse your anxiety; then I will become more afraid. Show me courage. I learn more from a model than a critic.

For years we have blamed the temperament of babies upon the ability or clumsiness of the mother. That argument started to dissolve as it became apparent that even the third or sixth baby was sometimes a "terror in the cradle," even though the mother by this time was really quite an expert. When a report was made recently to the American Academy of Pediatrics that each baby born has his own built-in style for reacting to life, a great deal of the prior blame that was once assigned to generations of guilt-ridden mothers was lifted somewhat. This does not mean, however, that the type of care and environment that is given an infant has no bearing on a child's disposition. It has, but not nearly to the degree formerly thought. Parents whose babies are especially difficult need to be assured that it would be wrong for them to shoulder the blame entirely. Out of 101 infants studied, eleven were rated difficult, forty-one easy, and forty-nine in-between. I hope you just had an easy one, or at least an in-betweener, but if you didn't, at least you alone are not to blame.

the discipline of duty

the sources of anger

180 An expert in child care recently said it was high time that parents talked back to children. She admitted that a certain amount of frustration is good for children. A loving home is not a place where every want and whim of the children are met. Parental demands and expectations, even when they are not entirely just, need to be heeded by children. What we need is a family-centered home, not a child-centered one. If this nation ever goes down the primrose path of family disintegration, I can only predict chaos and turmoil unmatched anywhere on earth. No children need or want an atmosphere in which everything goes. Family rules that are fair and flexible are an urgent necessity. It is important to listen to children. It is equally important that children listen to parents. It is perfectly natural for children to react with hostility to parental insistence. Any parent who doesn't buck his children sometimes is almost certainly doing something wrong. In a loving home the discipline of duty is indispensible.

Whether it is pleasant to admit it or not, humans are creatures of feeling rather than intellect—and therein lies the source of our anger. The chief source of anger is not frustration and aggression, but the discovery that we have to act maturely or unnaturally when our natural impulse is to behave selfishly or egocentrically. When children discover that their pleasures are limited by reality, then they become angry. Nevertheless, children as well as adults need to learn to cope with anger, their own and that of others'. It is good for a child to know why his mother is angry. Little good is done for the child when parents hide their sources of anger. Children need to know exactly what it is that angers their parents. The worst thing that can happen to a child is to be made the object of anger when an adult is really angry at something else. Parents ought never to take out their anger on their children, because children cannot cope with that indirectness. Humor can help children to vent their anger, and its liberal use should be encouraged—not laughter at the child, but with him.

neighborhood bully

the worth of stress

The neighborhood bully is not an unusual phenomenon. Handling that child is not a simple matter. Too often parents give their children strict orders not to be bullied, and to fight back at whatever the cost. For many children who are intimidated by bullies, standing up to the bully is not as simple as their parents make it seem. For one thing, parents of bullied children rarely want to take the issue to the parents of the bully because they don't want to damage adult relationships. This is the height of hypocrisy. On the one hand, we ask a little child to stand up to a bully, and on the other hand, his parents refuse to stand up to the parents of the tormentor. Here are some things to do about the bully in your neighborhood: First, bar the bully from your house and yard. Next, meet with his parents and state your case. Third, don't force your child to make a Custer-like stand; he may not be physically or emotionally ready to stand fast and fight. Fourth, allow your child to retreat to the safety of his home even if you personally feel humiliated.

For many years psychologists have been studying stress and its effects upon physical and emotional health. A list of forty-three life events has been devised that places each disruption of the normal life routine in its proper place according to its impact upon the physical and emotional welfare of the recipient. Try out your knowledge of human stress, and in the next second try to guess what event in a human's life is the most stress-producing event. If you guessed that it is the death of a spouse, you are correct. The scientists assign 100 points to this event. If in any one year you accumulate 200 or more impact events, then you are well advised to lie low and get help fast. If a man retires, sells his house, buys a condominium, and moves to Florida all in the same year, he will accumulate over 109 points. If he borrows some money, separates from his wife, and becomes ill himself, he will have 244 points, or enough to really do him in. Where the lives of children are involved in these impact events, one can guess that they will be affected by the physical and emotional disturbances of their parents.

children in disturbed families

when children die

182 Too often in families where there are serious problems, such as an alcoholic parent or a mentally disturbed father, the children are left out in the cold, surrounded by a thin veil of silence about the family problem. Except in the rarest of instances, children are reasonably aware that something is not right at home. Rarely are children so uncomprehending that they are taken by surprise by what appears to be obvious trouble in the family constellation. Adults who are well-intentioned attempt to shield the children, and thus they attempt to shut out reality. However, the child knows that all is not well. Youngsters who are not allowed to share the problem in accordance with their maturity level tend to feel left out of the family and even to magnify the problem out of proportion to its severity. Children can live with family handicaps provided they have enough knowledge to start to whittle away at the problem in their own fashion or with help. "Okay, Dad drinks. It is no fun. We need to live with it and help him." This attitude demonstrates how forthright an adult can be without destroying the security of children.

There is nothing more tragic than the death of a child. What parents who have suffered this agony need most is a chance to openly talk about their hurt, their loss and sorrow. Instead, all too often they meet with well-meaning friends and neighbors who talk about everything else but the passing of the child and the sorrow of those who remain to mourn. None of us likes to face the idea that our own child may be next, and so in our ignorance and fear, we avoid any mention of the tragedy to the parents who have so suffered. Recently in England a society was formed to bring together parents who have experienced the death of a child or who are presently in the throes of such agony. Parents who cannot share grief with others who understand often suffer both guilt and rejection of those children who remain. In an attempt to heal the wounds, some have other children; still others turn against the ones they have. As heartbreaking as a child's death is, its effects can be lessened through help from intelligent and compassionate friends.

help for the reconstituted family

mentally ill parents

As my class at the university has been graphing the problems of families who, because of death or divorce, remarry and have to bring up each other's children, we have become conscious of the fact that it is the feelings of these parents about each other and about their respective children that cause most of their problems. It becomes evident that man and wife must form a coalition, an alliance, that unites them in a broad range of common goals—easily prescribed but difficult to practice. Children not naturally related to their mother or father have strong feelings, both conscious and unconscious, about the parent to whom they do not belong. Worse still is the feeling each parent has, secretly or openly, about his or her natural children in this new marital relationship. Examining the underlying causes, while valuable as a study, does not always make much difference in the improvement of the problem.

Picture this scene if you can. Over a period of time a child has seen his mother retreat again and again into long hours of solemn silence. She sometimes sits and stares blankly at the walls until one day she is taken away the victim of mental illness. It seems obvious that prolonged contact with such a person will damage the emotional health of a child. Since in at least one in a thousand families one of the parents is hospitalized for a mental illness, there must be many children left at home in some rather precarious situations. Yet studies show that at least 40 percent of the children of psychotic parents are invulnerable to the almost predictable effects of a parent's emotional illness. Roughly 15 percent of these children do develop a psychosis, and nearly 50 percent become juvenile delinquents, but fortunately a surprisingly large group grow up normal. In fact, nearly 10 percent develop into superior, gifted children. The tentative conclusion at this moment is that there is a genetic factor still unknown that causes some children of mentally ill parents to crumble.

adopted children more trouble if they're adopted?

Whenever one talks about adopted children, tender feelings are developed in some listeners. It is a great thing to adopt a child, yet the achievement is not without danger. As the adopted child grows, his search for his own identity, for his feelings of being an inhabitant of a special place on earth, is no less intense than the search for this feeling of significance that all children go through. But adopted children have a difficult time, because while they are usually told they are adopted, they are rarely, if ever, told anything truthful about their natural mothers and fathers. Their biological ancestry is important to them; yet that information is fraught with embarrassment. The Committee on Adoptions of the American Academy of Pediatrics rightly recommends that at certain ages and stages, especially at the onset of adolescence, children need to know more about their biological parents than we often are willing to tell them. We can reduce the pain of growing up adopted with some judicious use of this genealogical information.

Are you bound to have troubled children if they are adopted? The results of a twenty-year study of sixty adopted and nonadopted children concludes that for the most part, disturbances need not occur more frequently in adopted than in nonadopted children. I have doubts about this conclusion, and even its wording seems to be somewhat faulty. This much is clear as we examine the conditions under which adopted children must live: it is only logical that when you have been chosen by one set of parents, you have at one time been rejected by another set. Otherwise you would never have been adopted. This is a severe fact to cope with at any age. Today we believe that when a child wants to know about his real mother or his real parents, he ought to know something about them. Frequently there is a seeking-out desire that is acted on by the child. If he has been told more about his parents, he may not find it as urgent to look for them. If he feels angry about the rejection by his natural parents, this should be expected and allowed. Who wouldn't be? Adoptive parents who are secure in their role can raise fine children, and they do.

what mothers know

family stimulation

I learned of a case the other day that will, I think, give all parents and educators some much-needed information about the identification of retarded learners. A kindergarten child was tested, after the fashion of the school, by the school psychologist. The school was worried about the little girl in question. She seemed bright enough, but she made some rather serious errors in her intelligence test. Not only did she make the error once, but she made similar errors as they continued the questioning. Now mothers love their children and often cannot see the trees for the forest, but it is also true that no one knows a child the way a mother does, particularly if that mother is an intelligent, observant human. And this mother knew her daughter was brighter than the test showed. Suspecting more than meets the eye, the mother decided to give the child a thorough physical exam. The result: her physician discovered that the child couldn't hear too well and thus misheard most of the intelligence tester's directions.

Very few failures in school have anything to do with a lack of brains or intelligence. Most failures in school are due to either emotional or social immaturity. We develop at our own pace. Each of us is born with a built-in time mechanism that conforms to no one else's—nor does it in any way resemble that of our brothers, sisters, or neighbors. Maturity for children has much to do with the social stimulation a child receives from adults who care for him. Too many people buy children every toy in the world, every type of schooling, summer camp, or vacation privilege, and still immaturity can retard learning. Parents need to buy less and attend more to their children. We need to show children what the good life is, not tell them how to make life good. The most up-to-date play materials will never take the place of stimulation that comes through deep and personal family involvement. Too often we breathe relaxed sighs when the children are quiet and off our hands. Off our hands—too often off our hearts.

the exceptional child   unloved children

186 While teaching a class recently in a very small town in my home state, I had the opportunity to invite a panel of mothers of handicapped, often called exceptional, children to meet with us. I was particularly interested in their personal feelings about the particular condition of their children. In summary I would say that all these mothers felt that their children who were not exceptional had strong feelings about their brothers and sisters who were. In general, until puberty this feeling was very positive and supportive. With the onset of adolescence, some of the positive feelings started to diminish. I am virtually certain of the fact that no mother can raise a singularly different child without some strong, overprotective feelings. I recollect making the comment that while many professionals in the field of exceptionality feel that this overprotectiveness is harmful to the overall growth and development of the child, it is great to know that there is someone who cares enough to fight tooth and nail for the welfare of that child. Were it not for some feisty parents, none of what we accept today in the education of these children might have been possible. Moderate overprotection never hurt anyone. Some call it love.

It was encouraging to learn that child-care centers are part of the curriculum in forty high schools in Massachusetts. National statistics indicate that in the first few years after high school, a large number of people have their first child. To those who still believe that everything a child needs is found naturally and plentifully in those who bear him, all I can say is that the evidence runs contrary to this view. In fact, too many parents neither love nor even like their children. Children who are genuinely unloved and are in homes where there is open hostility and even dislike from the parent are able to cope with this reglect better than those children who are unloved but whc are treated to double messages. This means that on the surface, and especially before outsiders, there is love from the parent. Below this there is a strong dislike for the child that shows persistently and often, thus telling the child on one hand that he is loved, but on the other hand that he really isn't. Learning to love children and to enjoy them can be taught, except to people with severe personality handicaps. And high school courses can help.

child beating

treating pain

Results of a study of the type of parents who physically abuse their children showed not that there was a particular personality trait about these parents, but rather that their educational level was the deciding factor. Let me clarify. When 30,000 child-abuses cases were studied, 67 percent of the persons who abused their children were on public assistance. Now it is true that parents on all socioeconomic levels believe it is their right to physically discipline their own children, but the poor are even more harassed by their children because of poor nutrition, poor and close housing, and a lack of alternatives to beating. Upper-income people can usually find a baby-sitter and run off to a local film or restaurant in order to escape their children. The poor have to grin and bear it—and they can't and don't. Equal opportunities for a satisfying life are very important in this matter, because parents who are unhappy in their lives tend to take it out on the kids.

Pain is a fearful thing to all of us, and a child's reactions to pain are largely determined by the adults with whom he lives. It is generally agreed that pain is more painful to children, but his parents' psychology about pain makes a great impression upon him, and he reacts accordingly. For example, if his parents are people who accept pain as part of the life they lead and do not whimper or become hysterical over it, then it is likely that they will be a model that will influence his reaction to pain. People who dramatize pain or who glory in it will transmit these values with a certainty. I found it interesting to discover a very real relationship between a person's occupational status and his reaction to pain. Office workers and professionals who rarely experience pain because of the nature of their work tend to overreact to cuts and bruises, while farmers, athletes, and construction workers who experience pain frequently are more likely to pass pain off as just a part of everyday life. Children need to know that pain hurts and that reaction to it is normal. Extremes in reaction teach the child an unnatural way of life.

when children cheat

fire!

188 Cheating, in and out of school, has always been a problem. A child cheats when the stakes for success are so high that he dare not fail. When expectations are beyond the pale of possibility, when life or death seems to depend upon success in a test, then in a very real sense we have driven people to cheat. And the home is often the place where childhood cheating is encouraged, albeit somewhat subtly. When parents don't actually discuss cheating, when they don't take a stand on the side of not cheating, when they cheat themselves and their children know it, then we can be virtually certain that cheating will occur. Cheating often stems from homework that is never checked, when homework is piled on to the point of absurdity, when children are afraid to ask for help, and when tests don't accurately test learning.

No one thinks we ought to frighten children unnecessarily, but there is wisdom in families sitting down together and planning calmly and intelligently what they will do if fire breaks out in their home. Doing what comes naturally in a fire is usually the wrong thing to do. Instinct doesn't serve us too well when flames are roaring about. Here's why: It is quite natural to race out of a room toward a hallway in a fire. Yet fire often races through halls, and so it is important to figure out *two* ways out of every room, especially the bedrooms. In the event that fire is in the hall, children need to know another way they can get out of their rooms. Upper-story rooms are a problem, of course, so children need to learn how they can climb out of a window, onto a roof, out to a tree, or down a ladder. Be sure everyone knows enough never to return to a burning house from the outside until the fire department has said it is safe. Once out, stay put, even though you may feel safe enough to make one last dash in. Finally, practice drills pay off. Forget the valuables. Save the people!

drugs and parent models

parents and drugs

It comes as no surprise to anyone that children who use drugs are more likely to come from homes where the parents are especially liberal, particularly rejecting of traditional values, and in general what you might call mod all the way around. At Stanford University a research team of fairly permissive, avant-grade, hip-type people were not only shocked but dismayed by their own findings. A study of 101 families showed that families with solid, old-fashioned values that support children who repudiate drugs, families who govern their children's lives fairly carefully with regard to their friends, church attendance, discipline, food, study habits, and bedtime, have the lowest drug use. The study concludes that parents teach and children become like them. The high-risk parents believe that children need freedom and little tutelage. A Toronto study found that children who use drugs regularly tend to have parents who use drugs too. A two-year study of 8,500 Toronto high schoolers showed that drug-taking is a form of learned behavior. Super-mod parents may produce super-drugged kids.

Here are some tips to parents on youngsters and drug usage. First, remember that your patterns of drug usage serve as a model for your children. Repeated studies have shown a clear correlation between the degree of responsibility exerted by the parents and that exercised by the children. Second, curiosity and the frantic search for experience is a normal aspect of the adolescent growth process. Third, parents must discourage initial drug use. Too often by the time parents get all wound up over drugs, it is after the child has had too much experience. Finally, parents, not the schools or the churches, must assume full responsibility for the detection of the response to the drug use of their children. If parents do discover that their children are on drugs, it is a family responsibility to seek help. The child is not diseased; the entire family is. Hysteric emotion is not the response most likely to generate any real dialogue about seeking help. If discussion is carried on with reasonable maturity, there is a better chance to get to the central issues.

"games" children play

children and dirty words

Children learn many ways of battling their parents. One device that is used to control parents is behavior of the child that seems to say, "I will melt or break if you even look at me the wrong way, so don't." Too many parents are cowed by the long faces, moans, and sad looks of their children who have been chastized for bad behavior. Now there are some supersensitive children; there is no denying this fact. But supersensitivity is partly hereditary (undoubtedly from your spouse) and partly learned. In other words, when a child learns (and he often learns accidentally) that his parents are afraid to hurt his feelings, he may end up using this against them. If sulking, crying behavior achieves the desired effect upon his parents, he has learned another game to use in his repertoire of behavior. Sensitive children need to be dealt with fairly or else parents run the risk of teaching them that since they are easily hurt they have a beautiful excuse for living in the world doing whatever they please to whomever they care to hurt. A child's development is blocked when parents cater to sensitivity too much.

When children play games with their parents, they frequently lie or ask to do completely impossible things. A favorite game of children is called by one writer "shockie." In this game children will, in front of their parents, use the most vulgar language they can muster just to see what it can do to the placidity of the home. The usual parental reaction is to recoil in sheer horror and lace into the children. Let's examine some of the possible child motivations for playing "shockie" and how to manage them. When a three-year-old comes home from the park and has heard a popular four-letter word that is unthinkable in the regular vocabulary of anyone but a junkie, we may be sure that he has no idea what it means, and so his using it is meaningless. If a parent overreacts in this case, he reinforces the value of the word for the child, who is liable to use it again to get a similar reaction. In another case a thirteen-year-old does the same thing, eagerly awaiting the gasps of horror and indignation from his mother. What does a parent do?

when children play "shockie"

hyperactivity and parents

What does a parent do who has just heard some gutter language repeated by his thirteen-year-old, who can't wait to see the look of shock on his parent's face? An unexpected reaction, one of calmness and politeness toward the youth's newfound threat to family stability, is often sufficient to throw him completely off guard. Not holding one's head, not ranting and raving, but rather calmly asking for the meaning, usage, and derivation of the word is the parent's correct response. Parents need to be sure that they don't use any "shockie" words themselves. If they don't, then their reaction needs to be the same as it is in the case of back talk. Vulgarities need to be met with a parental response that, instead of retaliating or demanding apologies, tells the child that you understand he must be pretty angry to talk that way. And you can't just leave it at that; if the parents don't back talk and use irregular language themselves, then they need to say they disapprove and they need also to convey the feeling that they understand the child's anger.

A child whose behavior is marked by overactivity, overexcitability, impulsiveness, and a short attention span is called hyperactive. The search for its cause has been fruitless. I am impressed with a recent study by Dr. Dennis Cantwell at the University of Southern California who discovered, as he studied fifty boys diagnosed as hyperactive and fifty regarded as normal, that nearly one-half of the hyperactive youngsters had parents who also were either hyperactive or emotionally disturbed. From this statement it is difficult to conclude that hyperactivity is genetic. It is entirely possible, and even probable, that the effect of living in a home with parents who are either hyperactive or emotionally disturbed is the major cause of a child's hyperactivity. It is also within the realm of reason to suggest a genetic cause. A closer look at the parents of hyperactive children showed alcoholism, hysteria, and amoral or antisocial behavior to be common among the parents. Hyperactive children *and* their parents need help.

"only" children children need adults too

192 While the only child in the family enjoys many of the benefits of the undivided attention of his doting parents, analysts conclude that sooner or later he may begin to wonder why he is the only child in the family. At a meeting of the Western Psychiatric Institute, Dr. Jacob Arlow indicated that it is not uncommon for only children to develop fantasies and guilt feelings about their being the cause of no other children being born. At first only children to develop fantasies and presence of more children who will threaten their dominance in the family. Later on they somehow magically conclude that they have been the cause of other children not being born. A study revealed that many only children in families feel so guilty that they tend to have overlarge families of their own. Others develop irrational fears of anything that even suggests birth. Some become hypochondriacs, and others problem eaters. Many parents have worries about the loneliness and over-protection afforded only children, but few are concerned about the child's silent musing over his solitary state. A simple parental explanation about the reason for having one child is usually sufficient to stop the anxiety.

If you've had the impression that a child's peer group is unimportant, I must reverse that idea and say that I fully approve of the peer group influence and even pressure, but I hasten to add that a child learns his moral and character development more from adults than from age-mates. Setting children off in a total child's world is not the best way to socialize him. I make particular reference here to day-care centers and the like, which are often merely havens for children and their play. I have never talked disparagingly about play. I am saying rather that play is urgent and influential, but any child society cut off from the influence of an adult world is a rather dismal, animal-like existence. Nothing horrible will happen to a child deprived of the opportunity to play with others for some protracted periods of time. Rather, the child without consistent and sustained periods of time with adults is more likely to be annoying than the former. Parents, adults, and children need to grow together and not side by side in insulated communities.

listening to children

on competition

Though this may seem strange to you, expert therapists have discovered that being listened to is in and of itself a therapeutic experience for the person who is doing the talking. There is an art to listening. Too often I have heard children in trouble tell me that their parents never really listen. Parents especially can't seem to listen without interrupting and either defending or chastizing. A significant part of helping is realizing that the person in trouble needs to be fully heard. I cannot emphasize too much how vital it is that parents listen to children until they are completely through or until they indicate that that is all they wish to say. And the development of this art should start in very early childhood when we tend to give our children only fleeting moments of attention. Try this in your very next conversation with a child—try listening right through to the end of what he has to say. Not so simple.

Many of the things we plan for children are based upon what I like to call the myth of competition. I am for competition. I am for competition as long as certain conditions prevail. Notice, for example, that those who extoll the great virtues of competition tend to be those who have succeeded in it. Competition is motivation only for those who see that they have a chance of winning. Many who have depressed images of their abilities see only threat in competition; it is challenging only to those who have had a great many successful experiences. To others who are losers, competition is, in fact, very threatening. It is not how competition seems to the parent or teacher, but rather how the weaker of the competitors sees the competition; and consider that when competition is too important, children will do nearly anything to achieve the ends. They will cheat, steal, and lie to win. In football they play dirty. In tennis I have seen grown men of high intellectual and moral stature call good balls out. If "dog eat dog" becomes a way of life, then too many lambs are devoured.

193

foster parents   epilogue

194 At the National Conference of Foster Parents, Dr. Edward Zigler said, "Society expects you to be a saint, a parent, a psychologist, and an expert in mental health, but it doesn't provide you with the help you need or the deference you deserve." Foster parents are those people who, for a multiplicity of reasons, open their homes up to children who, for whatever reason, cannot live at home with their natural parents. There is no question but what there are innumerable examples of people who are really great foster parents. A couple in one city who had three children of their own took in two retarded bed-wetters and brought them along so that they could enter school and be reasonably assured of some success. But all is not so rosy. Many children in our society are housed with inadequate foster parents. Some are packed into foster homes where the motivation is solely monetary. Worst of all, there are too many children who, having been separated from their parents, never find a good foster home and are in familial limbo for years upon end. A real childhood is every child's right.

There have always been and will always be famed last messages to children. Lord Chesterfield wrote one. Polonius also wrote to tell Laertes what the world was all about. Walter Lippman years ago said this: "What is left of our civilization will not be maintained, what has been· wrecked will not be restored by imagining that some new political gadget can be invented, some new political formula improvised. Our civilization can be maintained and restored only by remembering and rediscovering the truths, and by reestablishing the virtuous habits upon which it was founded. There is no use looking into the blank future for some new and fancy revelations of what man needs. The elementary principles of work, and sacrifice, and duty, and the transcendent criteria of truth, justice, and righteousness, and the grace of love and charity are the things which have made men free." Let your children know that the drug cop-out and the alcohol escape hatch do not free, but bind men and keep them locked in what James Agee called our "corridors of despair."

index